Air Pollution Damage
to Vegetation

Air Pollution Damage to Vegetation

John A. Naegele, *Editor*

A symposium sponsored by
the Division of Agricultural
and Food Chemistry at the
161st Meeting of the
American Chemical Society,
Los Angeles, Calif.,
March 31–April 1, 1971.

ADVANCES IN CHEMISTRY SERIES **122**

AMERICAN CHEMICAL SOCIETY

WASHINGTON, D. C.   1973

ADCSAJ 122 1–137 (1973)

Library of Congress Catalog Card 73–85001

ISBN 842–0183–8

PRINTED IN THE UNITED STATES OF AMERICA

Advances in Chemistry Series

Robert F. Gould, *Editor*

FOREWORD

ADVANCES IN CHEMISTRY SERIES was founded in 1949 by the American Chemical Society as an outlet for symposia and collections of data in special areas of topical interest that could not be accommodated in the Society's journals. It provides a medium for symposia that would otherwise be fragmented, their papers distributed among several journals or not published at all. Papers are referred critically according to ACS editorial standards and receive the careful attention and processing characteristic of ACS publications. Papers published in ADVANCES IN CHEMISTRY SERIES are original contributions not published elsewhere in whole or major part and include reports of research as well as reviews since symposia may embrace both types of presentation.

CONTENTS

PREFACE

Air pollution is a fact of contemporary life. It is now recognized as being deleterious to vegetation and, in particular, to agricultural vegetation throughout the United States, Canada, Mexico, Africa, and Europe (1). Every major city in the United States suffers deteriorated air quality caused by increased industrialization and transportation. Unfortunately, the biological effects of *mal air* are not clearly understood even though the problem of contaminated air has been of social concern and attracted community attention since the 13th century.

Early concern about pollution, however, centered about suspended particulates, particularly those associated with smoke and soot as a result of fuel combustion for comfort and cooking. As coal became the fuel of choice for home and a developing industry, the problem became more complicated because sulfur dioxide became a major constituent of smoke. By about 1600, sulfur dioxide was recognized as a principal air contaminant, and as the metallurgical industry grew, so did the problem of sulfur dioxide. As the chemical industry developed in the early 19th century, hydrogen chloride, hydrogen sulfide, nitrogen dioxide, and hydrogen fluoride were found in increasing quantities in the air, along with other fumes from the increased production of heavy metals, including beryllium. Recently the complex of photochemical smog components, introduced primarily *via* the internal combustion engine, have commanded our attention because of their ubiquituousness and their increasingly obvious effects. The character of the air pollution problem has changed from one of relatively simple composition of carbon particulates to the exceedingly complex and variable photochemical smog of gaseous composition. The problem has thus changed from a local issue to one of world-wide status and from a visible nuisance to an invisible plague.

The severity of the air pollution problem becomes obvious as we learn to recognize the effects of aerial toxicants upon biological systems. The aesthetic degradation of the air by a pall of smoke is obvious, but the toxic subtleties of SO_2, heavy metal, or ozone are not as easy to recognize and evaluate. Establishing repeatable cause/effect data in regard to air pollution effects has been a principal problem in the area of human health effects. Fortunately, cause and effect data are obtainable in plant investigations, and even with our current limitations on symptomatology it is possible to obtain repeatable dose-related cause and effect data.

Plant toxicology does not yet have the advanced insights of human and animal toxicology. Consequently, the visible and most obvious gross effects on sensitive tissue have been the most studied and reported. The symptomatology syndrome arising from exposure to a relatively high concentration of a toxicant has been traditionally called an acute response and has occupied most of the attention of investigators studying vegetative effects. Most of these expressions of toxicity are general responses evidenced by pigment changes in the leaves, necrosis, or malformed growth. The shape, consistency, and location of these lesions are considered diagnostic, and they have been a helpful first order of magnitude estimate of the effect of air pollution on vegetation. Using these acute symptoms, many estimates of economic damage have been calculated and the presence of a phytotoxicant established.

Recently, however, in addition to the acute response of individual plants or plant varieties, an increased awareness of the symptomatic expression of low level toxic exposure for longer periods of time has developed. Often included in the literature of acute symptomatology, this so-called hidden injury was considered to be different from acute injury. This hidden injury was the early recognition that symptomatology and dosimetry were not clearly understood. When ozone and other photochemical oxidants became the object of intensive study, the response of plants to low-level long-term exposure to toxicants established a better understanding of the complex dosimetry and response of plants to toxic exposure. These studies have clarified the significance of chronic exposure and have, in turn, led to a better understanding of the complexity of dosimetry and plant response.

The complexity of plant response to toxicants is even more apparent as biochemical information regarding toxicosis has become available. However, the biochemical information has arisen from individual studies and reflects the interests of many investigators and many points of view. The appreciation of and recognition of the basis of biochemical lesions as responses to air pollutants is essential if we are to progress in this important field.

An increased awareness of the complexity of plant response also developed as considerations of the response of populations of plants exposed to a toxicant were initiated. Detailed descriptions of acute responses and even chronic responses were the result of chamber studies of individual plants held under relatively constant experimental conditions with only dosimetric variables. As investigators became more adept at recognizing symptomatology, whole fields of damaged plants were investigated, and the population aspects of the response became evident.

The presence of extremely susceptible and resistant clones led to controlled breeding for resistance. This resulted in population manipulation to produce resistant varieties. As the symptomatology of ozone injury became better known in crop plants, an increased awareness of ozone damage to trees developed. It was noted that mountainsides covered with vegetation were slowly being adversely and selectively affected and changed by photochemical constituents in the air in a subtle manner that contrasted dramatically with the widespread and complete removal of plants associated with point sources of SO_2. Thus it became demonstrable that wholesale and widespread population shifts could be affected by the subtle selection effect of toxic substances in the air. This, in turn, led to greater emphasis upon the population as a means of mediating change and produced further understanding of the complex nature of the biological systems that were responding to the increased contamination of the air.

The study of plant population toxicology is mandatory if we are to understand and eventually to ameliorate the problem of toxicant-mediated changes to the world around us. Rather than just being an interesting phenomenon to be studied by a few plant pathologists, the fact that toxic air can threaten our food supply stimulates us to greater concern. We still depend upon plants to exist. Phytotoxic response among many individual plants and plant populations is a fact, and adverse effects on food production are a matter of record. The papers in this volume address themselves to the problem.

Intrinsic to understanding the problem of air pollution is the necessity of understanding the chemical basis of the air pollution problem. If we are to have any grasp of the real effects of air pollution, much less predict future effects with any confidence, we must know the specific compounds involved, have some idea of their toxic nature and residence time in the atmosphere, and make some reasonable guess as to what the future composition of the atmosphere might be with respect to these phytotoxicants. For this reason Edward Schuck discusses the chemical basis of the air pollution problem.

Our appreciation of the magnitude and, in fact, the presence of air pollution problem on vegetation is rooted in our understanding of the acute responses of plants to toxicants. While this approach deals with only our initial appraisal of the problem, it has been a valuable tool and an important first step in understanding the dosimetry of toxic response in plants. O. Clifton Taylor discusses the variety of acute responses exhibited on a number of horticultural and agronomic crops.

As our experience with the air pollution problem grows, the subtleties of the problem become more apparent. They are expressed in response to long-term low-level exposures to toxicants, particularly the photochemical smog complex. William A. Feder reviews our current understanding of these responses.

Insofar as the response of plants to short-term high concentrations and the response of plants to long-term low-level concentrations of toxicants are expressions of the biochemical basis of plant response, Brian Mudd reviews the current status of the biochemical effects of pollutants on plants.

Since all this information is vital to developing an operational attack on the problem, Delbert C. McCune provides a summary and synthesis of plant toxicology to establish several possible schemes to organize our thinking and to provide a basis for future action.

The importance of the population as an entity of concern suggested the necessity of understanding how populations work to regulate change. This area of biology is now receiving considerable attention and holds the key to our understanding of how biological changes occur. Thus, James Harding discusses colonizing genetic populations as units of regulated change. This discussion naturally led to the question of how we manipulate populations to produce the kinds of changes that are of immediate help in alleviating the deleterious effects of the pollution problem. Hence, Edward J. Ryder reviews controlled selection for increased tolerance to air pollutants.

Populations can be likened to an organism with the various components linked to each other through the medium of chemicals. Insofar as this is a viable way to view populations, we would be amiss if we did not examine the implications of this concept when viewed with the disruption that the air pollution problem may initiate to community stability. To introduce this concept Michael G. Barbour discusses chemistry and community composition.

A viable example of the widespread and dramatic change that pollution can initiate on a plant community is found in the conifer forest of the San Bernardino mountains. This vivid example of what photochemical oxidants can do to initiate biological change provides an instructive base for future speculations. Paul Miller covers oxidant-induced community change in a mixed conifer forest.

Finally, our ultimate concern is the effect that air pollutants may have upon future agricultural production. Walter W. Heck summarizes the current views on this subject.

As you read this volume, we hope that you will appreciate not only the magnitude of the air pollution problem but also the complexity of the phenomena. In addition, we hope that you will become aware of the fact that the composition of the air we breathe is having an impact upon the plants we depend upon for food, fiber, and aesthetic enjoyment. Ultimately we hope that these realizations will stimulate you to use your professional and technical skills to ameliorate the problem.

1. Halliday, E. C., in "Air Pollution," World Health Organization, Columbia University Press, New York, 1961. This volume details more information on the history of the air pollution problem.

JOHN A. NAEGELE

Waltham, Mass.
May 1973

Chemical Basis of the Air Pollution Problem

E. A. SCHUCK

Statewide Air Pollution Research Center, University of California,
Riverside, Calif. 92502

Combustion of fossil fuels to release useful energy produces several gaseous and particulate wastes which are discarded into and temporally persist in the atmosphere. Many of these waste products undergo further reactions in the atmosphere to produce additional products. These emissions and their reaction products are detrimental to biological systems. The presence of these substances in the vicinity of urban areas has and will continue to exert detrimental effects on agricultural operations. Many sensitive crops can only be grown in areas far removed from urbanized areas. Many other crops while exhibiting little outward signs of damage suffer up to 50% reduction in growth rate and yields. Thus our energy based pollution problems are impacting in a substantial manner on agricultural land use planning and on costs of crop production.

Contamination of the air begins with the emission into the atmosphere of certain gases and particulates. This presentation briefly reviews the chemical nature of these emissions and their interactions in the ambient atmosphere. The first questions to explore are the reasons for the formation of these contaminants and why air pollution appears to be affecting ever increasing areas of the world. In this exploration, digression into fields other than chemistry is necessary in order to relate the chemistry involved to the overall pollution problem. Too restricted a viewpoint can be detrimental when examining the complex air pollution system. The chemistry involved, while fascinating, should not be viewed as a separate part of the system.

This discussion is restricted to the most common contaminants which affect the largest number of people. Therefore, attention is focused on the combustion process and its products. Such combustion is an oxidation reaction in which oxygen in air combines with a hydrocarbon fuel and results in the release of energy. The energy released is used for various purposes—*i.e.*, for heating homes, for automotive and aircraft propulsion, for generating electricity, for melting ore, etc. These combustion processes have at least three common characteristics: they release energy, all the commonly used fuels (wood, coal, oil, and natural gas) have as their major combustion products oxides of carbon and oxides of hydrogen [*i.e.*, carbon dioxide (CO_2) and water (H_2O)], and these combustion processes usually give rise to minor amounts of partially oxidized fuel such as carbon monoxide (CO), olefins, and unburned hydrocarbon fuel elements. In addition, the exhaust gases from combustion may contain oxides of sulfur (SO_x) which stem from small amounts of sulfur compounds in the supplied fuel. Oxides of nitrogen (NO_x) are also formed because of the high temperatures reached during combustion which promote the oxidation of the nitrogen contained in the combustion air. Particulate matter may also be present in combustion products, either from chemical processes occurring during combustion of because of direct fuel entrainment.

Since man today requires a large amount of energy for various reasons, he uses large amounts of fuel and therefore generates large amounts of combustion products which are discharged into the air. The energy demand is so great that each U. S. citizen is directly responsible—*via* his automobile, etc., or indirectly responsible because of his demand for electrical power and other products—for generating about 2–5 pounds of pollutants each day. When this individual pollutant output is coupled with the high population densities of urban areas, the daily emission of exhaust products into any given air mass reaches staggering proportions. The 7 million citizens of Los Angeles County, for example, emit about 3 million pounds of pollutants each day (*1*). Although the ventilating capacity of the atmosphere is large, it cannot cope with such an overload, and thus in and around urban areas elevated ambient concentrations of combustion exhaust products persist. This results in an air pollution problem since many exhaust products have direct and indirect effects on human health and welfare. We are being adversely affected by our own excretion products.

Curiously, it is the minor combustion products which cause the greatest concern since CO_2 and H_2O, which account for 80–95% of the products, are normal atmospheric constituents and are not presently considered to be adverse to health or welfare. However, some evidence suggests that the addition of CO_2 to the earth's atmosphere from combustion of fossil fuels may in the near future affect the earth's heat balance and drastically alter weather patterns (*2*).

The CO_2 problem is another subject, however, and attention is confined here to the localized effects of minor exhaust components. From a chemical standpoint there is a great deal of similarity among pollution problems in various U. S. cities since the universal use of combustion to fulfill energy requirements produces urban atmospheres containing the same exhaust components. Thus, each atmosphere contains, at a minimum, elevated concentrations of CO, olefins and other hydrocarbons, SO_x (mainly sulfur dioxide, SO_2), NO_x, and particulate matter. The ambient concentrations will be a function of many factors including source strength, source density, and local dispersion variables. From one area to the next gross variations will exist in the relative concentrations of these components which tend to hide the similarities of the problem. Between cities the relative ambient concentration is primarily related to the specific type of fuel used for heating and power production. In eastern cities these requirements are generally fulfilled by the use of oil and coal. Both fuels lead to the generation of more direct particulate matter and SO_x than does the use of natural gas. Natural gas, which is a more common fuel for heating and power production in the western United States, produces much less particulate matter and SO_x than produced by use of oil and coal. From a human sensory standpoint, the presence of large concentrations of SO_x and the direct particulate pollution in eastern cities tend to obscure the similarities to western city pollution. In all U. S. cities, however, there is one major combustion source of CO, hydrocarbons, and NO_x pollution which leads to nearly similar proportions of these three contaminants. That source, the automobile, accounts for 99% of the CO pollution, 40–80% of the hydrocarbon pollution, and 40–80% of the NO_x pollution. In fact, if we confine our examination to the downtown area of cities, the automobile contributions to hydrocarbon and NO_x pollution may exceed 90%. The contribution of automotive exhaust to SO_x and direct particulate emissions in urban areas is much more variable because of differences in fuel use and the degree of control.

Up to this point the discussion has concentrated on direct emissions of pollutants without regard to their recognized atmospheric interactions. Consideration of such interactions adds several new factors to the pollution problem since such reactions tend to increase the toxicity of the atmospheric mixture of contaminants substantially. Before proceeding to these interactions, consider the components discussed. Three of these, at the concentrations existing in many U. S. urban atmospheres, are directly detrimental to health and welfare: CO, SO_x, and particulate matter (*3, 4, 5*). The NO_x as emitted exists mainly as nitric oxide (NO), which inhibits the rate of vegetation growth and probably combines with human hemoglobin in a manner similar to CO. Nevertheless, no direct detrimental health effects have as yet been proved to be associated with ambient concentrations of NO. The major recognized problem is that certain atmospheric interactions rapidly convert NO to nitrogen dioxide

(NO_2). At present ambient levels in urban areas with more than 50,000 population, NO_2 has been shown to be producing adverse health effects (6).

Most of the hydrocarbons emitted in combustion exhausts are at ambient concentrations which are a factor of 500–1000 below those considered to have detrimental biological effects. There are, of course, exceptions to this rule. Benzo(a)pyrene is an exhaust product of coal combustion and is a known carcinogen. Ethylene, a major product of automotive combustion, is at high atmospheric concentrations in and near urban areas. This seriously alters the aging process in certain types of vegetation and results in large economic losses. The major problem associated with hydrocarbons is again related to atmospheric interactions which lead to generation of several new derivatives toxic to humans at observed ambient levels.

The atmospheric interactions which lead to the generation ot these new toxic species and which promote the rapid oxidation of NO to NO_2 have a common base. That base is related to the absorption of sunlight energy by NO_2 (6). Although most of the NO_x emitted is in the NO form, a small percentage of this contaminant exists after atmospheric dilution in the NO_2 form. NO_2 is an avid absorber of the ultraviolet sunlight energy which reaches the earth's surface. Such energy absorption is immediately followed by disruption of chemical bonds and the formation of two species, NO and oxygen (O) atoms. The O atoms instantly combine with air oxygen (O_2) to form ozone (O_3) which in turn instantly reacts with NO to re-form NO_2. This rapid cyclic reaction produces no overall change in the system and in the absence of competing reactions would not result in a net conversion of NO to NO_2 or in the observance of an elevated O_3 level. Certain hydrocarbons, however, can compete with oxygen for the O atoms and with the NO for the O_3. Although the rates of reaction with these hydrocarbons are a factor of 100 less than that of O atoms with O_2 and O_3 with NO, the net result over an hour or two is an unbalancing of the NO_2 photolytic cycle. The immediate observable atmospheric results are the steady conversion of all NO to NO_2, the formation of hydrocarbon oxidation products such as aldehydes and ketones, the steady building of elevated ozone levels, and the formation of hydrocarbon derivatives such as the peroxyacyl nitrates (7). In addition to these interactions of hydrocarbons with the NO_2 photolytic cycle, we also observe that some facet of this interaction promotes the rapid conversion of gaseous SO_2 to sulfur trioxide (SO_3) and thus by reaction with moisture to sulfuric acid (H_2SO_4) aerosols.

The effects of these interactions are indeed impressive. Consider a specific case. In Los Angeles before interaction the mixture is chiefly composed of relatively nontoxic levels of NO and hydrocarbons plus potentially toxic levels of SO_2. In a matter of hours interaction with sunlight has produced concentrations of O_3, aldehydes, peroxyacyl nitrates, and aerosols—all of which are detrimental to human health, cause eye irritation, and are damaging to vegetation and material products. Furthermore, at least one of the components, *i.e.*, SO_2, has undergone a change of state from a gas to liquid, which frequently severely limits visibility to less than 1 mile.

Previously it was indicated that direct particulate emission leading to visibility reduction and material soiling is a problem mainly in certain eastern cities. In contrast, direct particulate emissions in large western cities usually account for much less than 30% of the observed visibility reduction and soiling. Obviously the described atmospheric interactions involving SO_x are responsible for the bulk of these particulate effects. Since these atmospheric interactions occur throughout the lower atmosphere, their contributions to particulate problems in all other U. S. cities must also be substantial even though at this time the direct particulates are most important. In other words, elimination of direct particulate pollution in cities now suffering from such effects may do little to improve visibility problems.

The impact of atmospheric interactions can be realized by examining the air monitoring data in various cities. Records from Chicago, Washington, St. Louis, New York, Cincinnati, Denver, Philadelphia (8), and wherever air monitoring data are available, show the same evidence of atmospheric interaction as found in Los Angeles. Specifically the O_3 and NO_2 concentrations in all cities tested are well above the levels at which detrimental biological effects occur.

It might be concluded, based on this brief review, that enough is known about contaminants and their interactions to provide a clear basis for control. This is true only to a limited extent. The clearest guidelines for control are associated with the direct effects of specifically emitted contaminants. Elimination of CO, SO_x, and direct particulates should alleviate problems associated with these primary contaminants. The term eliminate does not include methods which merely change the nature of the problem. Tall stacks reduce local SO_x ground-level concentrations, but also permit layering of high concentrations which can come to ground level at points many miles distant and fumigate plants and animals. Furthermore, the SO_x emitted aloft eventually ends up as H_2SO_4, which changes the acidity of rainfall, resulting in other detrimental effects on our environment. Tall stacks only change the nature of the problem. At best they make the SO_x pollution more democratic and minimize localized health and odor complaints.

Another nonsolution is practiced at certain industrial locations which have an exhaust gas containing high concentrations of NO_2. Since this compound is highly colored and toxic, it causes complaints from local citizens. The solution is to set up an auxiliary combustion tower and convert the NO_2 to colorless NO which is less toxic and less odiferous. This solution might be termed the out-of-sight, out-of-mind approach. Again it solves nothing since atmospheric interactions guarantee that the NO will eventually be oxidized to NO_2.

Another debatable approach to pollution control involves the methods currently used to reduce hydrocarbons and CO in automotive exhausts. The need to control CO is based on its direct health effects while the need to control the hydrocarbons is based on their interactions with the NO_2 photolytic cycle which leads to elevated concentrations of NO_2, O_3, peroxyacyl nitrates, and aerosols. The solution adopted was to increase the efficiency of the combustion process, thereby reducing hydrocarbon and CO emissions. Unfortunately, the method adopted also leads to dramatic increases in NO emissions. When this increase in NO was objected to, the answer came back that increased NO in the atmosphere is beneficial since it rapidly reacts with and destroys ozone, one of the very health-related substances requiring control. This is another example of failure to view the total air pollution system. Of course NO destroys O_3, but one product of this reaction is NO_2 which is also detrimental to health. Furthermore, this NO_2 is the beginning point of sunlight absorption which leads to all the products of photochemical interactions. In a certain location excess NO will tend to reduce O_3 levels. However, downstream of these locations excess NO_2 will promote more photochemical reactions and perhaps even higher ozone levels. In part this nonsolution to automotive pollution may be a major cause of the substantial increases in ozone in many areas during the past few years. This automotive example clearly illustrates the need for in-depth analysis when plans are made to change any part of the system of air pollution. Decisions based on such an analysis are all the more important because the tradeoffs involve human health and welfare.

The examples above illustrate the difficulties and dangers of a myopic approach to air pollution control. What is required is a complete systems approach which takes into account all of the known direct and indirect interactions. Even this approach will have to be modified as new knowledge becomes available. It cannot be claimed, for example, that knowledge of all atmospheric interactions is complete nor that all known interactions have been assessed. Thus our attention has been focused largely on the most obvious and dramatic atmospheric interactions. Other less dramatic reactions also require further assessment. For example, aldehydes absorb sunlight energy and are capable of reactions leading to ozone formation

(9). These aldehyde reactions have been largely ignored since they are much slower and less effective than those now occurring. Yet, if these reactions are ignored, we may not be able to lower atmospheric O_3 values appreciably. One real and immediate problem facing the control engineer is the tendency for certain advanced automotive control systems to create aldehydes in the process of destroying hydrocarbons and CO. Should such systems be adopted without assessing the aldehyde problem properly, a new problem may be created in the process of solving an old one.

What is the role of aromatic hydrocarbons in atmospheric interactions? Here again these compounds weakly absorb sunlight energy. Although this absorption is generally not capable of bond disruption, these high energy state aromatics are capable of transferring this energy to oxygen. This transfer creates an excited oxygen molecule which can attack other hydrocarbons (10) in much the same way as O atoms and O_3. Another facet of aromatic hydrocarbons requiring attention is their suspected ability to form aerosols in the absence of SO_x (1).

These few examples show the desperate need for further research and assessment in the chemistry and all aspects of air pollution. One might question whether we have knowledge of all urban sources of hydrocarbons that are important to atmospheric interactions. Does all rubber dust from automotive tires remain as dust? What is the contribution of asphalt roadways to atmospheric hydrocarbons? Is the contribution from such unassessed and other unknown anthropogenic sources sufficient in itself to account for health-damaging levels of ozone? These and other questions require immediate attention if we are to realize the goal of effective pollution control.

Since this volume is concerned with air pollution effects on agriculture, it is appropriate to consider the relevance of this discussion of the chemical nature of air pollutants to agriculture. Many of the direct emissions and their atmospheric reaction products are detrimental to vegetation. Some, like the automobile exhaust product ethylene, speed up the aging processes in plants. Because of the presence of this compound in the air, it is most difficult to grow orchards in some urban areas unless they are grown in greenhouses and supplied with air from which ethylene has been removed. The effects of air contaminants on vegetation are indeed diverse. In contrast to the increased aging caused by ethylene, NO decreases plant growth in a nondestructive manner. That is, the plant will immediately return to its normal growth rate if the NO is removed from the surrounding air. Other compounds in the air such as NO_2, SO_2, O_3, and the peroxyacyl nitrates also reduce plant growth and crop yield by mechanisms not yet completely delineated. Exposure to these latter air contaminants is generally destructive to plant tissue, and thus recovery from exposure can only occur by replacement of the cells. In many instances where the atmospheric concentrations of such contaminants are in the tenths of a part-per-million range, the effects of exposure can cause complete loss of the crop. This is particularly true for Romaine lettuce, spinach, and certain tobacco species which are extremely sensitive to low concentrations of ozone and peroxyacyl nitrates. By far the most serious effect is the reduction in crop yield which, for certain crops, has been as high as 50%.

What then is the overall effect on agriculture? One effect is to restrict the kinds of crops that can be grown near large population centers. Romaine lettuce and spinach must be grown some distance away thus increasing production costs because of transportation. Many other crops grown near population centers experience increased production costs because of the decrease in growth and yield. It is quite apparent that discarding the waste products of our energy production into the air has forced many changes in agricultural land use planning and has contributed significantly to increased costs of crop production.

Literature Cited

1. Los Angeles County Air Pollution Control District data.
2. "Restoring the Quality of Our Environment," Report of the Environmental Pollution Panel, President's Science Advisory Committee, The White House, Nov. 1965.
3. "Air Quality Criteria for Carbon Monoxide," National Air Pollution Control Administration, 1970, AP-62.
4. "Air Quality Criteria for Sulfur Oxides," National Air Pollution Control Administration, 1969, AP-50.
5. "Air Quality Criteria for Particulate Matter," National Air Pollution Control Administration, 1969, AP-49.
6. "Air Quality Criteria for Nitrogen Oxides," Air Pollution Control Office, 1971, AP-84.
7. "Air Quality Criteria for Photochemical Oxidants," National Air Pollution Control Administration, 1970, AP-63.
8. Data from National Air Sampling Network and Continuous Air Monitoring Projects, Office of Air Programs, Environmental Protection Agency.
9. Altshuller, A. P. *et al.*, "Products and Biological Effects from Irradiation of Nitrogen Oxides with Hydrocarbons or Aldehydes under Dynamic Conditions," *Int. J. Air Water Pollut.* (1966) **10**, 81.
10. "Air Quality Criteria for Hydrocarbons," National Air Pollution Control Administration, 1970, AP-64.

RECEIVED September 23, 1971.

2

Acute Responses of Plants to Aerial Pollutants

O. C. TAYLOR

Horticulturist and Associate Director, Statewide Air Pollution Research Center, University of California, Riverside, Calif. 92502

Acute symptoms of injury from various pollutants in different horticultural and agronomic groups are visible on the affected plant. Symptom expressions produced include chlorosis, necrosis, abscission of plant parts, and effects on pigment systems. Major pollutants which produce these injuries include sulfur dioxide, peroxyacetyl nitrate (PAN), fluorides, chlorides, nitrogen dioxide, ozone, and particulate matter; minor pollutants are ethylene, chlorine, ammonia, and hydrogen chloride. Symptoms of acute injury are often used to identify pollutant source and to estimate agricultural damage.

Visible symptoms of acute injury have been the principal means of identifying the effect of air pollutants on plants for well over a century. They have served as major factors in assessing the impact of man's activities on the total environment and have served as the basis for numerous estimates of economic damage to agricultural crops. Such estimates are admittedly crude because the total effect of air pollutants on growth and development is not indicated by symptoms of acute injury. Nevertheless, such evaluations are essential since adequate controls historically develop only after economic pollutant damage is well documented.

Identification of specific toxic components of contaminated atmospheres can often be established by careful examination of the total symptom syndrome in a plant community. Many of the symptoms produced by a particular toxicant are sufficiently characteristic that positive identification of the causal agent can be made, but frequently recognition of the pollutant and identification of its source is a complex task. A variety of symptom expressions may be found in a single plant community because of differences in susceptibility among species and among individuals of a single species. Leaf tissue in various stages of development on a single plant typically varies widely in susceptibility. Relative humidity, light intensity, and other environmental conditions may affect sensitivity of leaf tissue thus causing considerable variation in the appearance of acute injury. However, an experienced observer with a knowledge of several disciplines of biological sciences can, after carefully considering the full symptom syndrome, usually provide a reliable evaluation of the pollution problem. Where fluorides and chlorides are involved, leaf analyses can be useful in supporting conclusions drawn from observations.

Leaves are the most active part of the plant in exchanging gases with the surrounding atmosphere, and they are the most vulnerable to acute injury. The leaves are covered with a waxy protective coating (cuticle); consequently, gaseous pollutants enter through open stomata in the same way carbon dioxide and oxygen are interchanged with the atmosphere. Toxic particulates are deposited on the surface of plant foliage and must either dissolve the cuticle or move through open stomata in a solution to produce acute injury. Occasionally fruits and blossoms are injured directly by air pollutants, but the prime target is the foliage.

Gas exchange by leaf tissue occurs primarily by diffusion through stomata and to a limited degree through mechanical punctures or cracks in the cuticle. After penetrating the cuticle and epidermis, gaseous toxicants encounter a water-saturated atmosphere in the intercellular spaces and an aqueous solution which bathes the cell walls of internal leaf tissue. Solubility of the gas plays an important role in determining whether it is readily absorbed by the cells (1). Those gases which react with water to produce acids are absorbed readily and are strong phytotoxicants. Conversely, such gases as carbon monoxide and nitric oxide have low solubility in water and a low level of phytotoxicity.

The most severe injury produced by air pollutants is usually expressed by the death of large areas of leaf tissue. The dead (necrotic) areas become dry and may turn various colors ranging from white or ivory to red or dark brown. The first evidence of injury from high concentrations of toxicant is usually a grey-green discoloration of the injured area. As the cell contents begin to leak into the intercellular spaces, the injured area may develop a dark green, oily, or water-soaked appearance and become flaccid. Green color is bleached by subsequent desiccation, and the flaccid tissue becomes dry and brittle.

In the strictest sense, acute means that a disease has a sudden onset, a sharp rise in intensity, and a short course. To some researchers in the air pollutant field the term is reserved almost exclusively for necrotic symptom expressions produced by very high dosages. In this report the necrotic symptoms are emphasized, but attention is also called to other symptoms considered to be acute.

Necrotic areas may appear on an otherwise normal appearing leaf, or they may be accompanied by varying degrees of yellow discoloration (chlorosis). Chlorosis may form a transition zone between completely dead and the healthy areas, or it may cover any portion of the living tissue. Chlorosis often develops in tissues which have accumulated an excessive but nonlethal amount of a particular toxicant. Various patterns and degrees of chlorosis occur when chlorophyll is attacked by the toxic pollutants. Characteristics of the chlorotic pattern are influenced by the sensitivity of plants exposed, type of pollutant, dosage received, and environmental conditions under which the plant is grown.

Leaves with symptoms of acute injury usually drop prematurely. Abscission layer development may be stimulated by a rapid reaction of leaves to a high concentration of toxicant, resulting in heavy defoliation without detectable necrosis or chlorosis. Exposure to very high concentrations of nitrogen dioxide, chlorine, or hydrogen chloride may cause extensive defoliation within a few hours. Much lower concentrations may cause gradual development of typical symptoms of senescence, followed by premature dropping of affected leaves.

Descriptions of acute injury produced by individual air pollutants are abundant in the literature (2, 3, 4, 5, 6, 7, 8, 9), and several review articles provide excellent summaries of these descriptions (6, 10, 11, 12, 13, 14). Color prints of symptom expressions considered to be typical for a particular toxicant have been included in several of the publications (5, 6, 9, 10, 11, 14). This paper is not an exhaustive review of the literature or a detailed description of all possible acute symptoms produced by the various pollutants. It is a synoptic report of acute pollutant injury on plants.

Necrosis

Sulfur Dioxide. SO_2 injury on plants has received much attention, particularly during the past half century, and the toxic effects are well known. Symptoms of acute injury to specific crops have been described by investigators in several countries (2, 3, 4, 6, 7, 8, 15). Acute necrosis results from rapid absorption of SO_2. Once SO_2 enters the mesophyll tissue, it reacts with water to produce the sulfite ion which has strong phytotoxic properties. When lethal concentrations accumulate in the most susceptible areas of the leaf, a dark green, water-soaked discoloration develops. The affected area soon becomes flaccid, and upon drying becomes white to ivory on most plants. In some instances the dead tissue may turn red, brown, or almost black.

Acute SO_2 injury on broad-leaved plants may develop marginal or intracostal necrotic areas. Tissue along either side of the major veins is usually not affected, making the veins stand out clearly on the ivory-colored, necrotic background. Sulfur dioxide will react with water after entering leaf tissue to form sulfite ions which are subsequently slowly oxidized to sulfate. Both sulfite and sulfate ions are toxic to plant cells, but the former is reported to be as much as 30 times more toxic than the latter (16).

Sulfite concentration increases rapidly with a high rate of SO_2 absorption (17). When this occurs, intercostal and/or marginal areas collapse and dry out, leaving regions that are ivory-colored or, in some plants, irregularly shaped, dark brown necrotic areas. Organic sulfates migrate to the leaf margin and produce marginal necrosis which may extend between the major veins toward the midrib. Bleached or chlorotic tissue may develop between the necrotic lesion and healthy appearing tissue.

Small grain crops such as barley, oats, rye, and wheat are relatively sensitive to SO_2 injury. Injury on these grain crops and other parallel-veined plants usually develops as necrotic streaks between the veins near the leaf tip and extends toward the base as the severity of injury increases. On grasses and grains where the long, limber leaf blade curves downward, injury is usually most severe at the bend.

Sulfur dioxide injury usually starts at the tip of pine needles and extends toward the base as successive exposures produce more severe injury. Young needles, produced during the current growing season, are more sensitive than older needles. High concentrations of SO_2 usually cause a water-soaked area which subsequently turns reddish-brown or orange-red. Injury may first appear as a dark band around the needle with the tip portion turning brown later. Successive exposure to injurious levels of SO_2 may then produce dark-colored bands on the brown, necrotic part of the needle.

Fluoride. Fluoride damage to plants has been observed and studied in Western Europe for well over a century, and during the past 50 years has received considerable attention in the United States (6, 10, 13, 17). Plant damage is attributed primarily to hydrogen fluoride (HF) contamination, but silicon tetrafluoride and other gaseous forms released by industry are also toxic. HF is much more abundant in polluted areas than the other fluoride compounds.

After penetrating the open stomata, HF is readily dissolved in the aqueous solution which bathes the internal leaf tissues. If high concentrations [greater than 3 or 4 parts per billion (ppb)] of the gas are present in the atmosphere, an acid-type burn will develop on sensitive tissue. Intercostal areas of the leaf first become water-soaked as the cell contents leak through the damaged cell membrane into the intercellular spaces; then after drying for a time, they turn brown or light tan. Transition from healthy tissue to necrotic lesion is abrupt. After several days the necrotic tissue on injured apricot, grape, and other woody plant leaves may separate from the remainder of the leaf and drop away, leaving a ragged hole.

Fluorides are readily translocated to the tip and margin of leaves in the transpiration stream. If atmospheric levels of HF are low enough, the intercostal injury will not develop, and the fluoride concentration will increase at the periphery of the leaf. Acute fluoride intoxication at the margin of dicotyledonous plants, according to Solberg *et al.* (*18*), is first characterized by a collapse of the spongy mesophyll and lower epidermis, followed by distortion and disruption of the chloroplasts of the palisade cells, and finally, distortion and collapse of the upper epidermis. The injured area soon turns brown during hot, dry weather, but this symptom may be delayed if the weather is cool and damp.

On iris, gladiolus, tulip, and similar plants susceptible to fluoride injury, a narrow, dark-colored band often separates the dead and living tissue, and a series of these bands will develop as new tissue is killed by continued accumulations of fluorides. Similar bands may develop on leaves of susceptible woody species, but the necrotic tissues may also break away in a few days, leaving an irregular leaf margin. The leaf seldom separates from the tree because of the injury unless extremely high atmospheric concentrations of HF have occurred.

Several species of pine and fir are considered to be among the most fluoride-susceptible plants. Needles of these coniferous trees are most sensitive to HF while they are elongating and growing rapidly in the spring. Necrosis starts at the tip and progresses toward the base as fluorides accumulate. The injured tissue becomes chlorotic and subsequently changes to reddish-brown or sometimes to a lighter shade of brown. One-year-or-more-old needles are seldom, if ever, injured by fluorides in the atmosphere.

Acute injury on parallel-veined leaves of monocotyledonous plants typically develops at the tip of the leaf blade. Repeated exposures to lethal dosages of fluoride will extend the necrotic lesion toward the base of the blade. Sometimes the lesions extend farther down the leaf margin than nearer the midvein, and often the lesion on one margin will extend farther down than on the opposite side. Living and dead tissue is usually separated by an abrupt line of dark-colored tissue. Successive fumigations often produce a series of these dark-colored bands.

Nitrogen Dioxide. NO_2, a product of combustion and certain industrial processes, may produce acute injury on plants. However, atmospheric concentrations seldom reach a level sufficient to produce acute injury unless an accidental release of NO_2 or of nitric oxide (NO) occurs. An occasional incident has been reported near industrial plants where large quantities of nitrogen oxides are released as by-products

Since nitrogen dioxide is soluble in water, it is readily absorbed when its enters the intercellular cavities of the leaf. With high atmospheric concentrations, absorption is rapid, and susceptible areas on recently matured and rapidly expanding leaves are killed. As with most of the other toxicants, irregularly shaped areas between the veins first become water-soaked, and after drying, bleach to a white or light tan with a consistency resembling tissue paper (Figure 1). Somewhat lower atmospheric concentrations may produce small, irregularly shaped, dark-pigmented lesions when susceptible plants are exposed for several hours. These symptoms often resemble ozone injury.

Susceptibility of leaf tissue to NO_2 injury is increased under conditions of low light or in total darkness. Comparable injury may be produced by one-half that amount of NO_2 in the atmosphere on a dark, cloudy day compared with a bright, sunny day. Apparently, a light-dependent enzymatic reaction will reduce nitrites produced from foliar-absorbed NO_2 to the ammonia form which is readily used as a plant nutrient. Under low light this reaction is suppressed, and toxic levels of nitrites are allowed to accumulate.

Ozone. O_3 is the principal oxidizing component in photochemically produced air pollutants. Ozone probably causes more injury to vegetation than any other pollutant in the United States (6). Phytotoxic levels frequently occur near industrial complexes and densely populated urban areas. Exposure for two or more hours to concentrations of 10 parts per hundred million (pphm) of air may cause acute injury to several of the most sensitive species of plants.

Recently expanded leaf tissue is most susceptible to ozone injury. Very young, rapidly growing leaves and older, matured leaves are quite resistant. From a single exposure of a few hours, symptoms of acute injury usually develop at the tip of the youngest injured leaf and spread over progressively larger areas on each of the three or four successively older leaves.

One of the earliest indications of ozone injury on several plant species is an upper surface discoloration with a waxy appearance. This symptom often disappears completely a few hours after exposure is terminated. High dosages of ozone cause permanent necrotic lesions on susceptible leaf tissue. Permeability of cell membranes is apparently disrupted, and cell contents are allowed to leak into the intercellular spaces producing a water-soaked appearance. Upon drying, the tissue will totally collapse and turn white or various shades of brown. Lesions which extend through the entire thickness of the leaf are commonly referred to as "bifacial

Figure 1. Nicotiana glutinosa *leaves with bifacial necrosis produced by 2.3 ppm NO$_2$ in an eight-hour exposure. Left: upper leaf surface; right: lower leaf surface.*

necrosis." The size of these lesions may vary from a few millimeters to several centimeters in diameter. The lesions may cross over major veins, particularly near the leaf margin, but the veins and some tissue along each side frequently survive, leaving a green strip extending through the necrotic areas.

Ozone may pass through the spongy mesophyll of leaves on deciduous trees and shrubs without causing injury and attack islands of cells in the palisade parenchyma (Figure 2). Examination of cross sections through such lesions on citrus and grape leaves indicates that the chlorophyll is destroyed and is replaced with a red to reddish-brown pigmentation. The upper epidermis and often an upper layer of palisade tissue remains intact and apparently healthy for a considerable period. From the upper surface of the leaf the small lesions can be observed as irregularly shaped, dark-colored dots or as discolored areas a few millimeters in diameter. These lesions cannot be seen from the lower leaf surface unless the leaf is held up to a strong light. The "stipple like" lesion may be red, purple, black, brown, or straw colored.

Ozone may cause severe tip burn on current season needles of sensitive pine species. Semimature needle tissue is most seriously affected. Pink lesions and bands may form on the ozone-injured needles, followed by a distally spreading, orange-red necrosis which may take one to two weeks to reach the needle tip.

Interveinal streaks of white necrotic tissue develop between the veins of small grains, grasses, and corn (Figure 3). The lesions may cross the smaller veins, and when the injury is very severe, it may even cross the

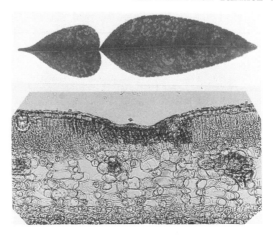

Figure 2. Upper surface necrosis on citrus leaf was produced by ozone in polluted ambient air. Fresh, non-stained section through an ozone-induced lesion on a citrus leaf. Dark region in palisade tissue collapsed several weeks after initial injury.

larger veins. The tip of young rapidly growing leaves is most severely injured, and usually a progressively greater area on the next two or three older leaves is equally sensitive. Heaviest injury normally occurs where the leaf blade bends downward.

Peroxyacetyl Nitrate. PAN, a highly toxic component of photochemical air pollutants, is responsible for serious plant injury in and near major urban centers. Acute injury is seldom observed on woody shrubs and trees, but many of the succulent ornamentals, grasses, vegetables, and weeds may be severely injured in a two-hour exposure by as little as 10 to 20 ppb.

Typically, PAN attacks spongy mesophyll tissue surrounding the substomatal chambers on the lower side of the leaf. When tissue immediately beneath the lower epidermis is killed, the epidermis dries, producing a glazed or bronzed appearance on the lower leaf surface. Usually there is no evidence of injury on the upper surface when the glazed or bronze symptom develops. Later, as the upper part of the leaf continues to grow, it cups downward, becomes rugose, and distorted.

Very high dosages of PAN will produce bifacial necrosis. A diffuse, transverse band across the leaf blade first appears water-soaked, then dries to produce a white to tan-colored necrotic band. Injury usually develops at the tip of week-old leaves at the base of the third or fourth older leaf and as a diffuse band across intermediate-aged leaves. The tip and base of the intermediate-aged leaf will remain free of injury.

PAN produces distinct bands on leaves of small grains, grasses, and corn (Figure 3). The band of white or occasionally dark brown necrotic tissue may be from a few millimeters to a few centimeters wide, depending on the size of plant and duration of the exposure. Large corn plants exposed for several hours may develop a wide band, while smaller plants and a shorter exposure will produce a narrow band. It often takes as much as 48 to 72 hours for the necrotic lesion to fully develop following an exposure. The major veins may survive, and the tip portion of the leaf may remain green and apparently healthy for an extended period.

Minor Pollutants. These often occur in polluted atmospheres of localized areas in sufficient quantity to produce injury on susceptible plants. Some of these materials are gaseous by-products of combustion—*i.e.*, ethylene and hydrogen chloride—while others such as chlorine and ammonia are waste products of industrial operations or are released accidentally to the atmosphere.

Figure 3. White necrotic fleck at tip of center leaf of Poa annua *produced by ozone. Transverse, necrotic band at midleaf was produced by peroxyacetyl nitrate (PAN).*

Injury by ethylene (ethene) typically develops slowly over a considerable time (chronic injury) and is expressed as distortion of growth, epinasty, chlorosis, defoliation, and excessive drop of blossoms or fruits. Symptoms of acute injury on orchid blossoms (dry sepal) may be produced by six-hour exposure to 0.1 ppm when the flower bud is in the most susceptible stage.

Accidental release of ammonia can cause very high concentrations to occur briefly in the atmosphere. In such instances leaves may show a cooked green appearance and may stay green or turn brown on drying (*1*).

Various types of necrotic spotting and streaking have been reported when different types of plant material were exposed to high concentrations of ammonia. Several cereals and grasses have shown necrotic and chlorotic interveinal streaking at considerable distance from an accidental spill. Red-to-purple pigmentation is often associated with the streaking on leaves of monocot plants. Upper surface glazing with or without scattered necrotic spotting has been reported.

Chlorine and hydrogen chloride (HCl) will produce acute symptoms on a variety of plants. Typically, a heavy dose of chlorine or chloride as an air pollutant will produce white to tan colored, irregularly shaped necrotic spots between the veins of leaves (Figure 4). In many ways the white necrotic lesions produced by chlorine and HCl on herbaceous plants closely resemble acute injury produced by ozone. Occasionally, glazing of lower leaf surfaces produced by HCl is similar to PAN injury. Chlorine and chloride injury on grapes, broad-leafed trees, and pine needles may sometimes be difficult to differentiate from acute injury produced by hydrogen fluoride. Analysis of leaf tissue is an effective means of determining which toxicant was responsible for the injury. Chloride analysis is less effective than fluoride analysis for identifying the air pollutant injury because most plants can accumulate excessive chlorides through the root system. Tissue analyses are ineffective for identifying effects of other pollutants because the toxicant is not accumulated in sufficient quantity to be detected or because the background level normally in the tissue is sufficient to mark that absorbed from the air.

Chlorosis

Most chlorotic symptoms are produced by long-term or repeated short exposure to relatively low concentrations of the toxicants and are generally considered to be symptoms of chronic injury. There are exceptions, however, when chlorosis appears in conjunction with necrosis following exposure to high concentrations of toxic pollutants. Slight differences in susceptibility of leaf tissue will determine whether a particular injured area will become chlorotic or will develop necrotic lesions. The chlorosis may develop independently or may appear as a border around necrotic lesions. Fluoride, for example, may produce chlorotic areas extending from the leaf margin between the major veins on citrus and sweet cherry leaves without evidence of necrosis. On corn, fluoride injury symptoms may be represented by a yellow mottle concentrated toward the tip of leaves and along the leaf margin toward the tip. The yellow-to-straw colored areas tend to be confined between the larger veins and are mostly concentrated toward the outer side of the interveinal zone. Chlorine injury on such plants as barley, radish, elm, and spinach frequently produces general bleaching and yellowing with no distinct pattern. The veins may be bleached by chlorine almost as readily as the web between veins with no evidence of necrosis.

Ozone may cause extensive chlorosis during an exposure of two to four hours to concentrations as high as 40 to 50 pphm. A general bleaching of mature leaves on melons, squash, beans, and radishes frequently develops after exposure to a heavy dose of ozone. Chlorotic "flecking" or "streaking" of corn, small grain, and grass leaves may also develop after relatively brief exposure to high concentrations of ozone. Injury on

Figure 4. Bifacial, intercostal necrosis on almond leaves produced with a four-hour exposure to 0.5 ppm chlorine

sensitive pine needles characterized by chlorotic "mottle" may develop first at the tip and with repeated exposures spreads farther toward the base of the needle.

Leaf Drop

Extremely high dosages of NO_2 or chlorine for a few minutes may stimulate rapid leaf drop with no identifiable chlorosis or necrosis. Under field conditions, accidental spillage of chlorine has been observed to cause almost complete defoliation of eucalyptus and elm trees within a few hours, even though the exposure lasted only a few minutes. In controlled experiments, NO_2 caused excessive defoliation of citrus, peppers, and other deciduous plants when they were exposed briefly to very high concentrations (250 ppm). Ozone-induced leaf drop may result from brief exposure to high concentrations, but more often it results from long-term or repeated exposures and probably should be considered a symptom of chronic injury.

Symptoms of acute injury are frequently used to identify pollutant sources and to estimate dosage. These symptoms are considered characteristic of the pollutant particularly when they occur on species known to be susceptible to the toxicant. A skilled observer must be able to differentiate these symptoms from injury produced by plant diseases, nutrient imbalance, climatic stress, insect feeding, or soil-borne toxicants. The symptom syndrome may be further complicated by a variety of less characteristic acute and chronic symptoms in the plant community. Systematic field observations provide one of the most valuable means of evaluating an actual or potential air pollution problem, but the observer should recognize the complexity of evaluating the various symptoms which may be encountered.

Literature Cited

1. Hill, A. C., *J. Air Pollut. Contr. Ass.* (1971) **21** (6), 341–346.
2. Benedict, H. M., Breen, W. H., *Proc. Natl. Air Pollut. Symp.*, *3rd, Pasadena,* *1955,* 117–190.
3. Danes, R. H., *J. Occupational Med.* (1968) **10,** 84–91.
4. Guiderian, R., *Schriftenr. Landesanstalt Immissions Bodennutzungsschutz Landes* (1967) **4,** 80–100.
5. Hindawi, I. J., *Natl. Air Pollut. Contr. Admin., Publ.* **AP-71,** 1–44 (1970).
6. Jacobson, J. S., Hill, A. C., Eds., "Recognition of Air Pollution Injury to Vegetation: A Pictorial Atlas," *Air Pollut. Contr. Ass., Air Pollut. Contr. Admin., Inform. Rept.* **1,** A1-H3 (1970).
7. Linzon, S. N., *Forest Chronicle* (1965) **41,** 245–250.
8. Linzon, S. N., *J. Air Pollut. Contr. Ass.* (1966) **16,** 140–144.
9. Van Haut, H., Stratmann, H., *Schriftenr. Landesanstalt Immissions Bodennutzungsschutz Landes* (1967) **9,** 50–70.
10. Brandt, C. S., Heck, W. W., "Effects of Air Pollution on Plants," in "Air Pollution," A. C. Stern, Ed., Vol. 1, 2nd ed., pp. 401–443, Academic, New York, 1968.
11. Middleton, John T., Crafts, A. S., Brewer, R. F., Taylor, O. C., *Calif. Agr.* (1956) **10** (6), 9–12.
12. Thomas, M. D., Hendricks, R. H., "Effects of Air Pollution on Plants," in "Air Pollution Handbook," P. L. Magil *et al.,* Eds., Section 9, pp. 1–44, McGraw-Hill, New York, 1956.
13. Thomas, M. B., in "Air Pollution," *World Health Org. Monograph Ser.* **46,** 233–278 (1961).
14. Darley, E. F., Nichols, C. W., Middleton, J. T., *Cal. Dept. Agr., Bull.* (1966) **55,** 11–19.
15. Matsushima, J., Harada, M., *Bull. Faculty Agr., Mia Univ.* (1964) **30,** 11–32.
16. Thomas, M. D., Hendricks, R. H., Hill, G. R., *Ind. Eng. Chem.* (1950) **42,** 2231–2235.
17. Thomas, M. D., Alther, E. W., "Handbook of Experimental Pharmacology," Vol. 22, pp. 231–306, Springer, Berlin.
18. Solberg, R. A., Adams, D. F., Ferchau, H. A., *Proc. Natl. Air Pollut. Symp.,* *3rd, Pasadena, 1955,* 164–176.

RECEIVED October 30, 1972.

3

Cumulative Effects of Chronic Exposure of Plants to Low Levels of Air Pollutants

WILLIAM A. FEDER

Suburban Experiment Station, University of Massachusetts,
240 Beaver St., Waltham, Mass. 02154

The biological effects of repeated exposure to low levels of air pollutants can be studied using green plants. Plants exposed to 10 ppm ozone over a long time show reduced growth, leaf size, stem length, root weight, and flower production, as well as a delay in the onset of floral initiation. These effects are expressed in terms of the depression of total plant growth or population growth, as distinguished from acute effects which generally cause injury to plants or plant parts but do not necessarily affect total growth or productivity. Attempts to measure the impact of air pollution on agricultural productivity must consider both the acute and the cumulative dose response relationship.

The precise difference between so-called acute and chronic effects of air pollutants upon plants is difficult to define but could be regarded as one of dose rate (exposure time and concentration) rather than one of symptom expression. The expression "hidden injury" has been used over the years. However, its value as a descriptive term has been carefully evaluated by McCune *et al.* (*1*), who have not found the term useful. It may be more correct to talk about chronic exposure instead of chronic symptoms since the time at which the symptoms appear after fumigation does not necessarily affect their characteristics.

Experimentally, investigators have tended to expose plants to relatively high concentrations of pollutants for periods of less than 24 hours. These exposures generally cause varying amounts of plant injury at the subcellular, cellular, and tissue level, and the resultant visible symptomatology is used to describe the quality and the severity of the injury. As described by Taylor (*2*), different plants react with different intensities to each pollutant and pollutant level. This allows us to ascribe different threshold levels of sensitivity to different pollutants for each plant type tested.

Under field conditions, plants are generally suspected of being pollution sensitive if some visible symptoms of injury can be correlated with the presence of a particular pollutant or group of pollutants in the air. A plant growing in its normal habitat is usually exposed to a fluctuating level of one or more pollutants. This level may exceed or at any time fall below the level demonstrated to cause injury to the particular plant species or type exposed to the same pollutant under laboratory conditions.

The problems with which this paper deals are whether, to what extent, and how a plant is altered when it is exposed for protracted periods to levels of pollutants below the recognized threshold at which visible injury symptoms occur. The exposure may be steady or intermittent but must continue for a long time at a low pollutant concentration.

That plants are affected by chronic exposure to low levels of certain pollutants has been known for many years. A number of authors have recognized this phenomenon (2–14): Stoklasa (3), Haselhoff and Lindau (4), Holmes et al. (5), Hill and Thomas (6), Setterstrom et al. (7), Thomas and Hendricks (8), Thomas and Hill (9), Hull and Went (10), Koritz and Went (11), MacLean et al. (12), Menser et al. (13), Thompson et al. (14), and Taylor et al. (2).

Fluorides

When the cumulative load of fluoride in the plant reaches a threshold concentration, a number of characteristic symptoms may appear, culminating with death of the plant. The levels of fluoride in a plant may be high relative to the background amounts in the ambient air. The concentration at which injury symptoms appear seems to depend largely upon the plant species and to a certain extent upon a series of complex interacting environmental conditions which in turn affect the physiological state of the plant.

Fluoride levels can be determined in plant tissues by leaf, stem, or root analysis (15–17). Rates of accumulation can therefore be calculated by the relationship of plant tissue levels to ambient air levels in terms of exposure time (18–20). The accumulation of fluoride in plants is similar to the accumulation of heavy metals in biological systems. The chronic exposure of the plant to low levels of fluoride causes the plant to accumulate fluoride. This can be measured quantitatively, and the level can be related in a quantitative manner to the intensity of symptom expression.

Under controlled conditions, a number of workers (19–22) have shown that the foliage of plants exposed to regulated amounts of hydrogen fluoride in a closed system accumulated fluorine in proportion to the duration times the concentration of fluorine in the atmosphere. Fluorine in the leaves of sweet cherry trees was correlated closely with ambient fluorine under field conditions by Compton *et al.* (*15*). Plant injury is likewise cumulative as can be demonstrated in such plants as corn and sorghum where a chlorosis without marginal necrosis of the leaf develops. The discoloration is at first marginal, starting at the leaf tip, but increases in width, length, and intensity as the time multiplied by the concentration exposure increases (*15*).

Pasture grasses and small grains are symptom-free even at leaf concentrations of several hundred parts per million of fluoride. Thus, the absence of injury symptoms on a plant does not necessarily mean that this plant has not been exposed to a pollutant in the environment in which it is growing, and such a symptomless plant may actually contain high concentrations of a pollutant like F. The accumulated fluoride is not evenly distributed, but tends to accumulate in the leaf tips and margins (*18, 23, 24*). Tips of oat leaves may contain 10–100 times as much F as the basal portion (*15*).

MacLean *et al.* (*12*) found that a dissimilarity in the rate of F accumulation in timothy grass between continuous low and intermittent HF exposures was not reflected in fluoride-induced foliar markings at the end of the exposure period. They found no visible differences in the extent and severity of foliar symptoms.

Plants chronically exposed to low levels of fluoride can be shown to accumulate F in tissue with or without accompanying plant injury.

Sulfur Oxides

Stoklasa characterized hidden injury as that resulting from prolonged or recurrent low-level fumigation with sulfur dioxide, not manifested by immediately visible symptoms but by decreased growth, faster aging of foliage, accumulation of sulfates, and reduction in photosynthesis (*3*). The effects of recurrent or chronic exposure of plants to sulfur dioxide in the air are expressed as changes in rate of growth and total dry weight; *i.e.*, yield. Thomas and Hendricks (*8, 25*) used the rate of photosynthesis under low-level sulfur dioxide fumigations as a measure of chronic injury and concluded that when there was no visible injury, there was no chronic injury. This work was verified by Katz (*26*).

These data and those of others (*1, 5, 6, 26, 27*) indicate a change in growth rate and/or a reduction in leaf area after prolonged exposure to sulfur dioxide. These effects indicate possible alterations in the normal physiological functioning of the plant, and therefore probably have both a visible (ultrastructure) and biochemical basis.

Sulfur dioxide is not readily detectable in leaves as an inorganic residue. Thomas (25) found that plants whose leaves were exposed to sulfur dioxide accumulated sulfur in the form of sulfate and sulfite ions. The level of these inorganic ions in leaves may be related to leaf injury, but the evidence is not as clearcut as it is in leaves with accumulated fluoride.

Work with $^{35}SO_2$ by Thomas et al. (28, 29) and Furrer (30) indicated that leaves absorbed sulfur dioxide and that some of the label remained in the leaves in the form of inorganic sulfur ions, but a major portion of the label was systematically distributed throughout the plant. Zuckerman and Feder (31) showed that the label was rapidly eliminated from the plant through its root system. Thus, since there seems to be little possibility of measuring sulfur residues in plants after fumigation with sulfur dioxide, the effects of recurrent, chronic exposure of plants to low levels of sulfur dioxide must be measured first in terms of plant growth and ability to flower, fruit, and set seed. Alterations in these readily measurable activities will suggest changes in biochemical patterns and in ultrastructural characteristics which can then be investigated.

Thomas (32) and Katz (26) state that damage to the crop does not occur until 5% or more of the area of the leaves shows visible markings. The visible markings are the same as if the plant had been fumigated for a short time with a much higher concentration of the pollutant. This is not the type of injury which distinguishes chronic from acute, but it is a dosage–response relationship which introduces the concept of time. It is not chronic injury, but rather chronic exposure to low levels which will produce typical injury symptoms in most cases if the plant is subjected to the pollutant for a long enough period of time.

Costonis et al. (33) were unable to demonstrate a positive correlation between ambient sulfur dioxide levels and inorganic sulfur ion accumulation in the needles of pines which are injured by relatively low levels of sulfur dioxide in the air. White pines growing in air polluted with more than 0.25 ppm of sulfur dioxide are often stunted, and a direct correlation can be obtained between plant growth and ambient SO_2 levels (34). However, tissue analysis does not reveal a measurable rise in sulfur level as inorganic sulfate ions. It is posible that the excess sulfur is incorporated into cell protein, but the data conflict (28, 35). For these reasons, it is not possible to follow sulfur accumulation in plants chronically exposed to low levels of ambient SO_2 without resorting to labeled SO_2.

However, this does not preclude following the effects on plant growth of chronic exposure to low levels of sulfur dioxide. Injury is manifested in altered growth rates, reduction in plant size, and alteration in reproductive capacity, all of which are visible only if the plants can be compared with others of the same variety growing under nonpolluted conditions. A proper evaluation of the chronic affects of sulfur oxides on plants awaits the successful combining of field data with data obtained under more rigorous experimental laboratory and greenhouse conditions.

Photochemical Oxidants and Oxides of Nitrogen

These pollutants are truly transitory. Ozone and peroxyacetyl nitrate have very short half-lives and leave no trace in the plant tissues. Oxides of nitrogen are longer lived but are also not traceable once they enter the plant, except in terms of their effects. They cause visible injury symptoms on the leaves of plants providing pollutant dosages are above the injury threshold for the plant variety.

Injury can result from short-term exposure to high concentrations or from longer exposures to lower concentrations of the pollutant. Again the visible symptoms are the same, and there are expressions of growth and yield differences at the lower level longer exposures.

Using individual citrus trees which were exposed to clean or smog-polluted air, Thompson and Taylor (36) and Thompson et al. (37) were able to show a reduction in crop yield from trees growing in unfiltered air. They showed that the combined pollutants in smog caused reduced water use, reduced photosynthesis, increased leaf and fruit drop, and severe reduction in yield. All of these changes occurred without the appearance of any visible injury to the leaves or fruit.

Work by Thompson et al. (14) showed that when Zinfandel grapes were subjected to naturally occurring smog for 14 weeks in the field, their yield decreased. The leaf area, fresh and dry weight of canes, and leaves and weight of individual berries were all reduced on those plants growing in unfiltered, smog-laden air. Chlorophyll in micrograms per square centimeter showed a reduction of almost 50% in the smog-exposed grape vines. The reduced chlorophyll content diminishes photosynthetic activity and can probably explain most of the other effects noted by the authors. In this experiment, visible injury symptoms did occur on the vines which were subjected to smog in unfiltered air.

Another study conducted by Taylor et al. (2) revealed similar effects on Zutano avocado seedlings exposed to synthetic smog for 7 hours per day, 5 days a week for 8 weeks. The pollutant was a mixture of 1-hexene and ozone which was allowed to react in a glass reaction tube with the end product (synthetic smog) directed into the fumigation chambers. The average daily oxidant concentration was 0.17 ppm, and there was no free ozone in the system. It took 10 days at this dose rate for symptoms to appear on the leaves, and the symptoms became somewhat more severe with accumulated exposure time. There were marked effects on growth including a reduction of 56% in stem coloration, a 35% reduction in leaf area, a 56% reduction in stem weight, a reduction in root volume, and a 65% reduction in root weight.

This work indicated that exposure periods considerably longer than 14 hours were necessary at low pollutant concentrations to cause visible symptom expression. Thus, previous work by Todd (38) and Taylor et al. (2) using short-term exposures did not reveal the inherent sensitivity of this avocado cultivar to synthetic smog because the cumulative dosage of pollutant was not permitted to reach the injury threshold. Went and co-workers (10, 11) also report reduction in growth and yield when tomato, alfalfa, sugar beet, and endive plants grown in synthetic smog are compared with those grown in charcoal-filtered air.

Many of the effects that occur as a result of these fumigations can probably be attributed to a destruction of chlorophyll. Chlorophyll loss attributed to fumigation with ozone or ozonated hexenes has been described (37, 39, 40, 41) and can be used as a quantitative measure of injury to cultured plants by certain pollutants. However, in the case of NO_2, growth suppression of tomato and bean occur after exposure to 0.5 ppm NO_2 for 10–12 days with a concomitant greening of the leaves, indicating the possibility of nitrogen accumulation and no chlorophyll destruction by the pollutant.

Craker (40) and Feder and Sullivan (41) have been able to build a dosage response curve for Lemna (Duckweed) which relates the ozone concentration, length of exposure, and percent chlorophyll destruction on a fresh weight basis by using a Spectronic 20. This technique makes it possible to quantify injury caused by ozone and to relate this injury to a particular dose rate for any plant.

In extensive studies during the last few years, Feder et al. (42–46), Heagle (47), and Brewer (23) have been able to demonstrate that plant growth is suppressed when the plants are grown to maturity in air in which the ozone level is kept at 8–10 ppm.

Using duckweed, carnations, corn, petunias, marigolds, chrysanthemums, and turf grasses, these workers showed a reduction in growth rate, stem elongation, leaf area, general plant size, top and root weight, fruit and seed set, and floral productivity. Corn grown in pollutant levels not exceeding 10 ppm for 7 hours per day, 5 days per week, suffers a reduction of 30% in leaf area, 20% in stem length, 32% in ear weight, and 60% in the number of filled kernels per ear (48).

Poinsettias grown to maturity in air mixed with 10 ppm of ozone have smaller colored bracts and take 2 weeks longer to mature (49). Carnations and geraniums reflect the same kind of patterns. Poinsettias, chrysanthemums, carnations, and duckweed show no visible injury symptoms even though they suffer depressed growth and productivity. Corn,

Table I. Comparative Leaf Areas (cm²) of Corn and Geranium Leaves and Poinsettia Bracts

Plant	Average Leaf Area, cm	
	0.0 ppm of Ozone	*12 ppm of Ozone*
Corn	3600	2684
Geranium	201	180
Poinsettia	32.1 [b]	19.6 [b]

[a] Exposed 5.5 hours per day for 60 days to 0.00 and 12 ppm of ozone.
[b] Bract area.

geranium, *Lemna,* and petunias begin to show symptoms when the cumulative dose of ozone reaches the injury threshold, which differs for each kind of plant and can be considered a measure of that plant's sensitivity to a particular pollutant (Table I).

Work with duckweed and poinsettias indicates that as long as these plants are growing in the presence of low ozone levels, growth rates, etc. are reduced. As soon as the plants are removed to clean, ozone-free air, growth resumes at a normal rate, and the plant rapidly reaches its normal size and habit. Thus duckweed exposed to 10 ppm of ozone for 14 days and then removed to fresh air exhibits a spurt in frond and flower production which quickly brings the population up to the normal level (*44*) (Table II).

This same reversible response is also exhibited by growing pollen tubes taken from ozone-sensitive varieties of tobacco and petunias. If the ozone dose is low enough, *i.e.,* high level but short exposure, tube elongation ceases momentarily and the tip of the tube narrows. After this growth resumes, and within minutes the normal growth rate is resumed and the tube recovers its normal diameter (*45*).

If the ozone level is too low, nothing will happen. If the level is too high, elongation will cease and the tube will die. These events occur within a narrow dose range (5–35 ppm for 5–15 min) and can therefore be used to study the threshold levels of sensitivity for pollen of any variety. Other work has shown that relative sensitivity of pollen to ozone is positively correlated to the ozone sensitivity of the pollen parent (*43*). Sulzbach and Pack (*46*) have also demonstrated that pollen sensitivity to atmospheric pollutants may be a useful tool for screening plant materials to learn their relative tolerance to pollutants and to attempt to discover selection pressures that may be affecting plant populations.

Conclusions

Evidence is accumulating which indicates that plants may exhibit depressed growth and yield with or without overt expression of injury

Table II.   Delay in Floral Development of Several Plant Species Exposed
Daily to 0.0 and 10 ppm of Ozone for the Complete
Growing Period of Each Plant Species

| | Time to Flowering, Days | |
Plant	No Ozone	10 ppm of Ozone
Duckweed (Lemna)	11	15
Petunia	25	32
Carnation	120	150
Corn	30	37
Poinsettia	51	80

symptoms. There is, undoubtedly, a relationship between the dosage–
response curves describing acute symptom expression and those which
can be used to express suppression of growth and yield. The relative
sensitivity of petunia cultivars to ozone is the same whether it is expressed
as acute injury after short-term exposure to high dosages or growth suppression after longer exposures to lower dosages. However, it is not
possible to predict an effect on growth or yield based upon the extent
of acute injury as measured only by visible symptoms. As yet, we do
not have a good understanding of the relationship between cumulative
ozone exposure and short term exposure. If periodic ozone peaks are
responsible for most injury symptoms under field conditions, but cumulative ozone concentrations resulting from longer periods of low ozone
levels are responsible for the effects on yield, then it seems reasonable
that both conditions must be taken into consideration in explaining plant
damage and yield losses. This is not being done at present in developing
criteria and standards, and the almost total reliance on acute injury data
is perhaps misleading since standards may be set which permit enough
pollutant to accumulate in the environment to cause yield reductions
in agricultural crop plants. The need for predictive models and equations
is evident, but there is also a need for a better understanding of how
plants react when exposed for long periods to low levels of air pollutants.

Literature Cited

1. McCune, D. C., Weinstein, L. H., MacLean, D. C., Jacobson, J. S., "The
   Concept of Hidden Injury in Plants," *Science* (1967) **85**, 33.
2. Taylor, O. C., Cardiff, E. A., Mersereau, J. D., Middleton, J. T., "Effect of
   Air-borne Reaction Products of Ozone and 1-N-Hexene Vapor (Synthetic Smog) on Growth of Avocado Seedlings," *Amer. Soc. Hort. Sci.*
   (1958) **71**, 320.
3. Stoklasa, J., "Die Beschadigungen der Vegetation durch Rauchgase und
   Fabriksexhalationen," Urban and Schwarzenberg, Berlin, 1923.
4. Haselhoff, E., Lindau, G., "Die Beschadigung der Vegetation durch Rauch,"
   1903, Gebruder Borntraeger, Berlin.
5. Holmes, J. A., Franklin, E. C., Gould, R. A., "Report of the Shelby Smelter
   Commission," *U. S. Bur. Mines Bull.* (1915) **98**, 528.

6. Hill, G. R., Thomas, M. D., *Plant Physiol.* (1933) **8**, 223.
7. Setterstrom, C., Zimmerman, P. W., Crocker, W., "Effect of Low Concentrations of Sulphur Dioxide on Yield of Alfalfa and Cruciferae," *Contrib. Boyce Thompson Inst.* (1938) **9**, 179.
8. Thomas, M. D., Hendricks, R. H., "Effects of Air Pollution on Plants. Air Pollution Handbook," pp. 1–44, Section 9, 1956, McGraw-Hill, New York.
9. Thomas, M. D., Hill, G. R., *Plant Physiol.* (1937) **12**, 309.
10. Hull, H. M., Went, F. W., "Life Processes of Plants as Affected by Air Pollution," *Proc. Second Nat. Air Pollut. Symp.* (1952) 122.
11. Koritz, H. G., Went, F. W., "The Physiological Action of Smog on Plants. 1. Initial Growth and Transpiration Studies," *Plant Physiol.* (1953) **28**, 50.
12. MacLean, D. C., Schneider, R. E., Weinstein, L. H., "Accumulation of Fluoride by Forage Crops," *Contrib. Boyce Thompson Inst.* (1969) **24**, 165.
13. Menser, H. A., Grosso, J. J., Heggestad, H. E., Street, O. E., "Air Filtration Study of "Hidden" Air Pollution Injury to Tobacco Plants," *Plant Physiol.* (1964) **39**, Lviii.
14. Thompson, C. R., Hensel, E., Katz, G., "Effects of Photochemical Air Pollutants on Zinfandel Grapes," *HortSci.* (1969) **4**, 222.
15. Compton, O. C., "Plant Tissue Monitoring for Fluorides," in "Pollutant Impact on Horticulture and Man," *Hort. Sci.* (1970) **5**, 244.
16. Chang, C. W., Thompson, C. R., "Effect of Fluoride on Nucleic Acids and Growth in Germinating Corn Seedling Roots," *Physiol. Plant.* (1966) **19**, 911.
17. Jacobson, J. S., McCune, D. C., Weinstein, L. H., Mandl, R. H., Hitchcock, A. E., "Studies on the Measurement of Fluoride in Air and Plant Tissues by the Willard-Winter and Semiautomated Methods," *J. Air Pollut. Control Assoc.* (1966) **16**, 367.
18. Jacobson, J. S., Weinstein, L. H., McCune, D. C., Hitchcock, A. E., "The Accumulation of Fluorine by Plants," *J. Air Pollut. Control Assoc.* (1966) **16**, 412.
19. Adams, D. F., Applegate, H. G., Hendrix, J. W., "Relationship among Exposure Periods, Foliar Burn, and Fluorine Content of Plants Exposed to Hydrogen Fluoride," *Agr. Food Chem.* (1957) **5**, 108.
20. McCune, D. C., Hitchcock, A. E., Jacobson, J. S., Weinstein, L. H., "Fluoride Accumulation and Growth of Plants Exposed to Particulate Cryolite in the Atmosphere," *Contrib. Boyce Thompson Inst.* (1965) **3**, 1.
21. Hitchcock, A. E., Zimmerman, P. W., Coe, R. R., "Results of Ten Years Work (1951–1960) on the Effect of Fluorides on Gladiolus," *Contrib. Boyce Thompson Inst.* (1962) **21**, 303.
22. McCune, D. C., "The Technical Significance of Air Quality Standards: Floride Criteria for Vegetation Reflect the Diversity of Plant Kingdom," *Environ. Sci. Technol.* (1969) **3**, 720, 727.
23. Brewer, R. F., Guillement, F. B., Sutherland, F. H., "The Effects of Atmospheric Fluoride on Gladiolus Growth, Flowering, and Corn Production," *Amer. Soc. Hort. Sci.* (1966) **88**, 631.
24. Compton, O. C., Remmert, L. F., "Effect of Airborne Fluorine on Injury and Fluorine Content of Gladiolus Leaves," *Proc. Amer. Soc. Hort. Sci.* (1960) **75**, 663.
25. Thomas, M. D., "The Invisible Injury Theory of Plant Damage," *J. Air Pollut. Control Assoc.* (1956) **5**, 203.
26. Katz, M., "Sulfur Dioxide in the Atmosphere and Its Relation to Plant Life," *Ind. Eng. Chem.* (1949) **41**, 2450.
27. Thomas, M. D., *Annu. Rev. Plant Physiol.* (1951) 293.
28. Thomas, M. D., Hendricks, R. H., Hill, G. R., *Ind. Eng. Chem.* (1950) **42**, 2231.

29. Thomas, M. D., Hendricks, R. H., Hill, G. R., Jr., "Air Pollution Proceedings of the U. S. Technical Conference on Air Pollution," pp. 41–47, 1952, McGraw-Hill, New York.
30. Furrer, O. J., "The Amount of Sulfur Dioxide Absorbed by Plants from the Atmosphere," *Proc. Symp. Isotop. Plant Nutrition Physiol.* (1966) 403.
31. Zuckerman, B., Feder, W. A., 1970, unpublished data.
32. Thomas, M. D., 1961 World Health Organization, Monograph Series No. 46.
33. Costonis, A. C., Sinclair, W. A., "Ozone Injury to Pinus Strobus," *APCA J.* (1969) 19, 867.
34. Linzon, S. N., "Damage to Eastern White Pine by Sulfur Dioxide, Semi-Mature-Tissue Needle Blight and Ozone," *APCA J.* (1966) 16, 140.
35. Spaleny, J., Kutacek, M., Opilstilova, K., *Air Water Pollut.* (1965) 9, 525.
36. Thompson, C. R., Taylor, O. C., "Effects of Air Pollutants on Growth, Leaf Drop, Fruit Drop and Yield of Citrus Trees," *Environ. Sci. Technol.* (1969) 3, 934.
37. Thompson, C. R., Taylor, O. C., Thomas, M. D., Ivie, J. O., "Effects of Air Pollutants on Apparent Photosynthesis and Water Use by Citrus Trees," *Environ. Sci. Technol.* (1967) 1, 644.
38. Todd, G. W., "The Effect of Gaseous Ozone, Hexene, and Their Reaction Products upon the Respiration of Lemon Fruit," *Physiol. Plant.* (1956) 9, 421.
39. Erickson, L. C., Wedding, R. T., "Effects of Ozonated Hexene on Photosynthesis and Respiration of Lemna minor," *Amer. J. Bot.* (1956) 43, 32.
40. Craker, L. E., "Effects of Mineral Nutrients on Ozone Susceptibility of Lemna minor L.," *Can. J. Bot.* (1971) 49, 1411.
41. Feder, W. A., Sullivan, F., "The Effect of Ambient Temperature on the Sensitivity of Aquatic Green Plants to Low Levels of Ozone," 65th Annual Meeting of the Air Pollution Control Association, 1972, Preprint No. 72-158, pp. 1–8.
42. Feder, W. A., Campbell, F. J., "Influence of Low Levels of Ozone on Flowering of Carnations," *Phytopathol.* (1968) 58, 1038.
43. Feder, W. A., "Reduction in Tobacco Pollen Germination and Tube Elongation, Induced by Low Levels of Ozone," *Science* (1968) 160, 1122.
44. Feder, W. A., Sullivan, F., "Ozone: Depression of Frond Multiplication and Floral Production in Duckweed," *Science* (1969) 165, 1373.
45. Feder, W. A., unpublished results.
45. Feder, W. A., "Modifying the Environment," *HortSci.* (1970) 5, 247.
46. Feder, W. A., "Plant Response to Chronic Exposure of Low Levels of Oxidant Type Air Pollution," *Environ. Pollut.* (1970) 1, 73.
47. Heagle, A. S., Body, D. E., Pounds, E. K., "Effect of Ozone on Yield of Sweet Corn," *Phytopathol.* (1972) 62, 683.
48. Feder, W. A., "Chronic Effects of Low Levels of Air Pollutants upon Floricultural and Vegetable Plants in the Northeast," Annual Report, Public Health Service Contract No. PH 22-68-39, 1970.
46. Sulzbach, C. W., Pack, M. R., "Effect of Fluoride on Pollen Germination and Pollen Tube Elongation," *Phytopathol.* (1971) 61, 913.
49. Craker, L. E., Feder, W. A., "Development of the Inflorescence in Petunia, Geranium, and Poinsettia under Ozone Stress," *HortSci.* (1972) 7, 59.

RECEIVED January 19, 1972.

4

Biochemical Effects of Some Air Pollutants on Plants

J. B. MUDD

Department of Biochemistry and Statewide Air Pollution Research Center, University of California, Riverside, Calif. 92502

Properties of the air pollutants sulfur dioxide, nitrogen oxides, peroxyacyl nitrates, and ozone have been considered from chemical, biochemical, and physiological points of view. Physiological observations cannot demonstrate the chemical mode of toxicity. Chemical and in vitro biochemical studies may be irrelevant at the physiological level. Consideration of all three approaches indicates which hypotheses of toxicity are more plausible and suggests new areas of investigation.

There is now ample documentation of the effects of air pollutants on vegetation (1). Development of symptoms has been studied in the field and under experimental conditions, in the latter case both with single pollutants and with mixtures (2). Conditions which predispose or protect plants from pollutant damage have been examined (3).

However, in no case have such studies informed us of the chemical bases for the toxic reactions. Examinations of lesions in the field can lead to the identification of newly polluted areas and new pollutants. Experiments in the greenhouse and laboratory can determine the dose response in terms of pollutant concentration and duration of exposure. Physiological studies of intact plants can correlate metabolic changes with the development of toxic symptoms. If we are to understand fully the effects of air pollutants on plants, however, it is essential that we elucidate the biochemical mechanisms of their action.

An alternative approach is to study the reactions of pollutants *in vitro* and, having found the reactivity of pollutants with known biochemical compounds, attempt to assess the relevance of such reactions to physiological conditions. Such an approach depends on (1) a knowledge of the chemical reactions of the pollutants and the biochemicals, (2) an examination of the reactions of the pollutants with biochemical compounds *in vitro*, and (3) examination of the effects of pollutants on plants to see if the reactions examined in (2) can explain these effects. The approach taken here is to emphasize the types of reactions the pollutants can undergo, not only to afford understanding of observations made both *in vivo* and *in vitro* but also to indicate new possibilities for research. This method attempts to present the status of biochemical investigations of air pollutant toxicity and also suggests a framework for assessing future investigations. We shall, therefore, take four individual pollutants and discuss them from the points of view of chemical properties, *in vivo* effects and *in vitro* effects.

Sulfur Dioxide

Some of the reactions of sulfur dioxide are listed in Table I. In this and other tables the relative merits of whether air pollutants act either

Table I.   Reactions of Sulfur Dioxide

Reactions in Solution
  (a) $SO_2 + H_2O \rightarrow H_2SO_3$ $pK_1 = 1.76$ $pK_2 = 7.20$
  (b) $H_2SO_3 \rightarrow H_2SO_4$ $pK_1 = 0.40$ $pK_2 = 1.92$

Toxic Reactions
  (a) $RCOH + NaHSO_3 \rightarrow R(OH)CH - SO_3Na$ [a]
  (b) $RSSR + SO_3^{2-} \rightarrow RS^- + RSSO_3^-$
  (c) reactions with pyrimidines

Detoxification by Metabolism
  (a) $SO_4^{2-} \rightarrow SO_3^{2-} \rightarrow \times \rightarrow \times \rightarrow -S-$ [b]
  (b) $SO_3^{2-} \rightarrow SO_4^{2-}$ [c]

[a] Also reactions with quiones and $\alpha\beta$-unsaturated compounds.
[b] Enzymic sulfate and sulfite reductions; reductant requirement equivalent to $4NADPH + 4H^+$.
[c] Enzymic sulfite oxidation.

Table II.   Biochemical Effects

Effect	*System*	SO_2 *Concn*
Methionine oxidation	Horseradish peroxidase	2–5 mM bisulfite
Bisulfite addition to pyrimidines	Nonenzymic	1M bisulfite
Disulfide cleavage	Nonenzymic	0.2M sulfite
Sulfite oxidation	—	—
Sulfite reduction	Enzyme from spinach	1 mM sulfite

(a) directly with biological components in a gas–solid reaction, or (b) with biological components only after the pollutants are in aqueous solution are not considered. However, most of the available information relates to the second alternative.

Some of the effects of sulfur dioxide are attributable to its acidifying effects, either as sulfurous acid or, after oxidation, as sulfuric acid. In at least one case the ability to convert sulfite to sulfate has been correlated with resistance to toxicity.

Possible toxic reactions of sulfur dioxide are also indicated in Table I. The reaction of bisulfite with aldehydes has a classic position in biochemistry since Neuberg demonstrated in 1918 that the products of fermentation by yeast were altered by the addition of sodium sulfite, which caused the production of equal amounts of the bisulfite addition compound of acetaldehyde and of glycerol. This was concomitant with the blockage of conversion of acetaldehyde to ethanol. Addition compounds can also be formed with quinones and with α,β-unsaturated compounds. None of these reactions has been adequately assessed as a possible contributor to toxicity.

Reactions of sulfite and bisulfite with biochemical compounds are shown in Table II. Sulfite has been used frequently as a reagent for cleaving disulfide bonds in proteins (6, 9). Such a reaction may participate in the scheme of sulfur dioxide toxicity.

Recent studies have demonstrated reactions of bisulfite with pyrimidines. Addition compounds are formed at the 5,6-double bond of the pyrimidine (5). Mutagenic effects have been observed with phage λ (10) and with *Escherichia coli* (11). However, the concentrations of bisulfite used in these experiments were $1M$ or higher, and one wonders if such effects would be observed at the much lower concentrations that could arise by exposure of vegetation to SO_2-polluted air.

Sulfite and sulfate both can be metabolized by plant tissue. Sulfite can be oxidized to sulfate, and this ability may be correlated with resistance (7). On the other hand, sulfate can be reduced all the way to sulfide (8). Sulfur dioxide is generally considered to generate a reducing type of air pollution, but in terms of the latter pathway of metabolism it should

of Sulfur Dioxide *in vitro*

Comment	Reference
Superoxide dimutase inhibited both sulfite and methionine oxidation	4
Reversible in basic solution	5
Products are free thiol and *S*-sulfonate	6
—	7
Product sulfide	8

Table III.   Biochemical Effects

Effect	*System*	*SO_2 Concn.*
Chlorophyll degradation	Lichens	—
Chlorophyll degradation	Mosses	1–10 ppm 5–50 hr
Inhibition of photosynthesis	*Euglena gracilis*	5 ppm 1 hr
Lesions	*Alnus glutinosa*	1 ppm
$^{35}SO_2$ metabolism	(Tomato) *Lycopersicon esculentum*	—
Toxicity	Mosses and lichens	—

be considered as an oxidant (Table I). Several authors consider the toxic effect of SO_2 to be caused by lowering of the pH (Table III), but it has also been pointed out that susceptibility of mosses and lichens to SO_2 is greatest at low pH (17). This may be a function of the relative ability of anion and undissociated acid to penetrate the cells.

In spite of its long history as a known air pollutant, sulfur dioxide has received little attention from plant physiologists and biochemists. Attempts to assess the physiological relevance of some of the reactions listed in Table I would be appropriate.

Oxides of Nitrogen

When oxides of nitrogen come in contact with water, both nitrous and nitric acids are formed (18) (Table IV). Toxic reactions may result from pH decrease. Other toxic reactions may be a consequence of deamination reactions with amino acids and nucleic acid bases. Another consideration is the reactions of oxides of nitrogen with double bonds (Table IV). The cis–trans isomerization of oleic acid exposed to nitrous acid has been reported (19). Furthermore, the reaction of nitrogen dioxide with unsaturated compounds has resulted in the formation of both transient and stable free radical products (20, 21) (Table V). A further possibility has been raised in that nitrite can react with secondary amines to form nitrosamines which have carcinogenic properties (22). Thus, the possible modes of toxicity for oxides of nitrogen are numerous and are not exhausted by this short list.

The metabolism of nitrate and nitrite has received a great deal of attention by plant biochemists. Both anions are reduced to ammonia (24). The reductants required for the metabolism of nitrate and nitrite are nicotinamide-adenine dinucleotides (NADPH), and it may be expected that exposure of plants to oxides of nitrogen will cause the diver-

of Sulfur Dioxide *in vivo*

Comment	Reference
Attributed to acid effect	*12*
Greater toxicity at higher humidity. Ability to convert SO$_2$ to sulfate correlated with resistance	*13*
Respiration stimulated	*14*
At low SO$_2$, high photosynthetic rate and sulfur accumulation gives no damage	*15*
Conversion to H$_2$S and amino acids	*16*
Susceptibility greatest at low pH (3.2). No toxicity of H$_2$SO$_3$ at pH 6.6	*17*

sion of the reductants from normal uses. In photosynthetic tissue the reductant is required for the photosynthetic fixation of carbon dioxide. Nitrogen oxides or nitrite will lower the fixation of carbon dioxide (*25, 26*) (Table VI). The carbon dioxide fixation returns to normal as soon as either the exposure to nitrogen oxides is stopped (*26*) or all the nitrite in solution is reduced (*25*). Nitrite is much more toxic than nitrate. At nitrite concentrations which are just over the threshold of acetate metabolism inhibition, the inhibitory effect can be reversed by illumination (*27*). This result is consistent with the proposal that reduction by NADPH removes the nitrite. Also, inhibition of acetate conversion to lipid, which requires NADPH, is greater than inhibition of the synthesis of nonvolatile water soluble compounds, which does not (*27*).

Physiological observations indicate that low concentrations of nitrogen oxides will cause growth suppression without formation of lesions

Table IV.   Reactions of Oxides of Nitrogen

Reactions in Solution

(a) NO + NO$_2$ + H$_2$O → 2HNO$_2$ nitrous acid pK = 3.40

(b) 3NO$_2$ + H$_2$O → 2HNO$_3$ + NO

Possible Toxic Reactions

(a) RNH$_2$ + HNO$_2$ → ROH + N$_2$ + H$_2$O [a]

(b) RCH = CHR + NO$_2$ → RCH—CHNO$_2$R
                              •

Detoxification by metabolism

NO$_3^-$ → NO$_2$ → X → X → NH$_3$ [b]

[a] Deamination of amino acids and nucleic acid bases.
[b] Reductant requirement equivalent to 4NADPH + 4H$^+$. Normal utilization of NADPH, *e.g.*, CO$_2$ + Ru-di-P + 2ATP + 2NADPH + 2H$^+$ → 2 3-P-glyceraldehyde + 2ADP + 2P$_1$ + 2NADP$^+$ 2H$_2$O.

Table V.   Biochemical Effects

Effect	System	NO_2 Concn.
Interaction with un- saturated lipids	Monolayer of phospholipid	3300 ppm
Interaction with un- saturated lipids	Chloroform solutions of lipids	Solution saturated with NO_2

(28). This indicates that below a certain threshold concentration, the plant can protect itself against acute damage, but this is at the expense of normal anabolic processes such as carbohydrate synthesis.

Several interesting studies have been made of the reaction of nitrogen dioxide with monolayers of lipids at the air–water interface (23, 29, 30). The surface pressure of lipid monolayers increased when they were exposed to nitrogen dioxide introduced in the air above the layer or in the subphase (29). The increase in surface pressure was a function of the degree of unsaturation of the lipid. Such a result is consistent with the formation of derivatives suggested by Estefan et al. (20). These results could have important biological implications since biological membranes contain a high proportion of unsaturated lipid. So far there has been no work done to test directly the effect of oxides of nitrogen on biological membranes or to look for the expected derivatives of fatty acids. For cholesterol monolayers, exposure to nitrogen dioxide lowered the surface pressure, and this was ascribed to the formation of cholesteryl nitrate which migrated to the subphase (30).

Peroxyacyl Nitrates

Most information concerning the peroxyacyl nitrates refers to peroxyacetyl nitrate (PAN), and these remarks are directed to this member of the family. In aqueous solution, peroxyacetyl nitrate degrades rapidly

Table VI.   Biochemical Effects

Effect	System	Concentration
Inhibition of CO_2 fixation	Chlorella pyrenoidosa; initial pH 4.2	0.25 mM nitrate in reaction mixture
Inhibition of CO_2 uptake	Medicato sativa, Avena sativa	0–10 ppm 0–2 hrs
Inhibition of acetate metabolism	Chlorella pyrenoidosa; pH 6.5	25 mM nitrite
Growth suppression	Nicotiana glutinosa, Phaseolus vulgaris, Lycopersicon esculentum	0.5 ppm 10–22 days

of Nitrogen Oxides *in vitro*

Comment	Reference
At constant area the surface pressure is increased. No effect on saturated lipids	23
RCH = CHR + NO$_2$ → RCH–CHNO$_2$R	20

at all pH values but most rapidly at alkaline pH (*31, 32*). The products are acetate, nitrite, and molecular oxygen (Table VII). These products are relatively nontoxic; the toxicity of PAN cannot be attributed to nitrite since the damage symptoms are so different.

Possible toxic reactions of PAN include reaction with the sulfhydryl group of biological molecules (Table VIII). The reaction with glutathione appears to involve not only oxidation, mostly to the disulfide, but also acetylation (*34*). One cannot say that this is a general reaction of PAN with sulfhydryl compounds since there was no evidence for the formation of acetyl coenzyme A (acetyl CoA) when coenzyme A (CoASH) was treated with PAN (*36*). The disulfide was formed along with a variety of other products which may be in higher oxidation states. Enzyme inactivation is consistent with the reaction of PAN with sulfhydryl groups, but in certain cases (egg albumin) PAN does not react with sulfhydryl groups which are accessible to *p*-hydroxymercuribenzoate (*35*). The modified residues of the proteins affected by PAN have not been isolated and characterized. Attempts to observe the formation of either disulfides or S-acetyl groups were negative (*36*).

Reduced nicotinamides are readily oxidized by PAN (*31*). Since the products form cyanide complexes with characteristic UV spectra and also react in a predictable fashion with specific dehydrogenases, they have been characterized as the biologically active oxidized forms of the coenzymes (*31*). A different reaction of PAN is with ethylenic double

of Nitrogen Oxides *in vivo*

Comment	Reference
Inhibition greatest at acid pH (3.0); O$_2$ evolution less affected than CO$_2$ uptake. Both recovered when all nitrate was reduced	25
Threshold for inhibition 0.6 ppm	26
Overall inhibition reversed by light, but lipid synthesis still preferentially inhibited. No effect by equivalent concentrations of nitrate	27
Also increase in chlorophyll and leaf distortion	38

bonds. Here, epoxides are formed (41), and such a reaction in biological systems may cause significant changes in membrane permeability. A further possible reaction of toxicity of PAN is with nucleic acid bases (37); however, in this case low pH conditions were necessary to observe

Table VII.   Reactions of Peroxyacetyl Nitrate

In Solution

$$CH_3COO_2NO_2 + 2OH^- \rightarrow CH_3CO_2^- + O_2 + NO_2^- + H_2O$$

Toxic Reactions

(a) $CH_3COO_2NO_2 + 3RSH \rightarrow CH_3COSR + RSSR + H_2O + H^+ + NO_2^-$ [a]

(b) PAN + reduced nicotinamide $\rightarrow$ oxidized nicotinamide

Detoxification

(a) $CH_3COSR + H_2O \rightarrow RSH + CH_3CO_2H$ enzyme: thio esterase

(b) $RSSR + NADPH + H^- \rightarrow 2RSH + NADP^-$
enzyme: disulfide reductase

(c) higher oxidation states $\rightarrow$?

[a] Plus higher oxidation states

Table VIII.   Biochemical Effects of

Effect	System	PAN Concn
Oxidation of reduced pyridine nucleotides	Pure compound in buffered solution	100 ppm 1–5 min
Reaction with isocitrate dehydrogenase, glucose 6-phosphate dehydrogenase, malate dehydrogenase	Pure enzyme in buffered solution	100 ppm 1–5 min
Reaction with GSH	Pure compound in buffered solution	100 ppm 1–5 min
Reaction with hemoglobin	Pure compound in buffered solution	100 ppm 1–5 min
Reaction with CoASH	Pure compound in buffered solution	100 ppm 1–5 min
Oxidation of DNA, pyrimidines, and purines	Pure compound in buffered solution	1000–2000 ppm 0–90 min
Inhibition of polysaccharide synthesis	Particulate enzyme system from *Avena*	430 ppm 3 min
Oxidation of indoleacetic acid	Assayed by change in UV spectrum	1.3–2.6 ppm 6 hr
Inhibition of cellulose synthetase, phospho-glucomutase, UDPG pyrophosphorylase	Enzymes from *Avena* coleoptiles	100–400 ppm 2–6 min

reaction. Another reaction of PAN *in vitro* is with indoleacetic acid. Spectral changes show that while indoleacetic acid is oxidized by PAN, tryptophan is resistant (*39*) (Table VIII). Ozone readily oxidizes both of these compounds.

The biochemical effects of PAN *in vivo* have been examined (Table IX). PAN does lower the sulfhydryl content of bean leaves (*45*). The first damage visible by electron microscopy is in the stroma of the chloroplast (*43*). Enzymes of cellulose synthesis are inhibited, but one of these enzymes, phosphoglucomutase, was more susceptible *in vivo* than *in vitro* (*42*). This observation suggests that the metabolic activities of the cell may either protect an enzyme or make it more susceptible to the pollutant. An intriguing observation on the analogs of PAN is that their toxicity increases as the alkyl chain lengthens (*44*). This is also true of the property of eye irritation. Two suggestions can be made to explain these differences: (1) the higher analogs are more readily absorbed and (2) the plant is less capable of detoxifying the thioesters formed from the higher analogs. Our preliminary tests of the absorption of peroxyacyl nitrates and substrate specificity of plant thioesterases indicate that neither of the above suggestions can explain the original observations.

Peroxyacetyl Nitrate *in vitro*

Comment	*Reference*
Oxidized to biologically active form	*31*
Enzymes can be protected by substrates and cofactors	*33*
Products: disulfide and *S*-acetyl compound	*34*
No reaction with ovalbumin or RNase	*35*
Products: disulfide and higher oxidation states, but no *S*-acetyl. Products analogous to those obtained with H_2O_2	*35*
No reaction above pH 5	*37*
Inactivation also by IAA and *p*-hydroxymercuribenzoate	*38*
No effect on tryptophan	*39*
UDPG pyrophosphorylase not affected *in vivo*	*40*

Table IX.   **Biochemical Effects**

Effect	*System*	*PAN Concn*
Inhibition of polysaccharide synthesis	*Avena* coleoptiles	35–50 ppm 4 hr
Inhibition of phosphoglucomutase	*Avena* coleoptiles treated with PAN and enzymes assayed in subcellular fractions	35–50 ppm 4 hr pH 4.8
Chloroplast damage	Pinto beans (*Phaseolus vulgaris*)	1 ppm 30 min
Lesions on plants	*e.g.*, bean, petunia	0.014 ppm 4 hr
Decrease in SH content	*Phaseolus vulgaris*	1 ppm 30 min
Decrease in SH content, decrease in chlorophyll	*Chlamydomonas reinhardoi*	125 ppm 1–10 min.

Table X.   **Reactions of**

Effect	*System*	*O$_3$ Concn*
Oxidation of amino acids	pH 4.5 (acetate) pH 7.2 (phosphate) pH 8.6 (borate)	1000 ppm 1–10 min
Oxidation of nicotinamide	Phosphate buffer pH 7.0	5–100 ppm
Oxidation of unsaturated fatty acids	Suspensions in aqueous buffer	—
Oxidation of lecithin	Lecithin from egg yolk	1000 ppm

Table XI.   **Biochemical**

Effect	*System*	*O$_3$ Concn*
Inhibition of O$_2$ uptake	Plant and animal mitochondria	
Inactivation of lysozyme	Enzyme from hen egg white	
Inactivation of cataloase, peroxidase	Aqueous solution	0.5–10 ppm
Inhibition of phosphoglucomutase	From oat coleoptiles	300 ppm 4 min
Ribonuclease and avidin inactivation	Aqueous solution	1000 ppm 1–10 min
Inhibition of acetylcholine esterase	Enzyme from bovine erythrocytes	0–1 ppm

of Peroxyacetyl Nitrate *in vivo*

Comment	Reference
—	*38*
—	*42*
First damage visible in EM is stroma granulation	*43*
PPN and PBN[a] more toxic than PAN	*44*
Darkness lowers SH content of control leaves	*45*
Chlorophyll *a* is more susceptible than chlorophyll *b*	*46*

[a] PPN, peroxypropionyl nitrate; PBN, peroxybutyryl nitrate.

Ozone in Aqueous Media

Comment	Reference
Order of susceptibility: cys, met, try his, tyr, phe	*50*
Only the reduced form is susceptible. Oxidation product not biologically active	*51, 56, 57*
Products include H_2O_2 and malonaldehyde, no double bond conjugation	*52–54*
Aqueous suspensions more resistant to oxidation than hexane solutions	*55*

Effects of Ozone *in vitro*

Comment	Reference
Reversed by ascorbic acid and glutathione	*59*
No inactivation when only tryptophan residues 108 and 111 were oxidized	*60*
Moles of O_3/mole of enzyme for 50% inhibition: papain, 233; peroxidase, 36,400; urease, 30,300; catalase, 45,160. O_3 3–30 times more effective than H_2O_2	*61*
No inhibition of enzyme extracted after coleoptiles treated with O_3	*62*
RNase inactivation related to his oxidation. Avidin inactivation related to try oxidation	*50*
Nonlinear dose response	*63*

Ozone

Since the literature on ozone chemistry is enormous, readers are directed to earlier publications (47–49). Most of the chemical literature describes reactions of ozone in organic solvents, where ozonides are relatively stable and controlled degradation under reducing or oxidizing

Table XII.   Biochemical

Effect	System	O_3 Concn
Visible symptoms	Tobacco leaves	0.8–1.0 ppm 5 hr
Inhibition of starch hydrolysis	Leaves of cucumber, bean, Mimulus	0.05 ppm
Inhibition of NADH level and phosphorylation	Euglena gracilis	0.8 ppm 1 hr
Inhibition of photosynthesis, lowering of chlorophyll b content	Euglena gracilis	0.2–1.0 ppm
Stimulation of O_2 uptake	Euglena gracilis	1.0 ppm 1 hr
Decrease in glutamic acid, increase in α-aminobutyric acid	Leaves of tobacco, beet, corn, barley, and rye	1 ppm 30 min
Diminished SH content	Bean, spinach, and tobacco	1 ppm 0–60 min
Inhibition of respiration	Tobacco	0.6–1.0 ppm 1 hr
Chloroplast damage	Pinto bean	0.6–1.0 ppm 30 min
Changes in fatty acid content	Tobacco	1 ppm 0–1 hr
Inhibition of photosynthesis	Pinus ponderosa	0–0.45 ppm
Increase in disulfide	Phaseolus vulgaris	0.25 3 hr
Formation of malonaldehyde	Phaseolus vulgaris	0.25 ppm 3 hr
Accumulation of sterylglucoside and acyl sterylglucoside	Tobacco	
Disruption of polysomes	Pinto bean	0.35 ppm 20–35 min
Decrease of ribosomal SH	Pinto bean	0.3 ppm 20–50 min
Increase of free amino acids	Cotton	0.5–0.8 ppm 1 hr
Inhibition of photosynthesis and transpiration	13 different plant species	0.4–0.9 ppm 30–120 min

conditions can give high yields of the desired products. When ozone is considered as a toxicant in biological systems, we are forced to examine ozonizations in water and at approximately neutral pH. The reactions listed in Table X are confined to such conditions.

Ozone reacts with several amino acids (50) (Table X). In some cases the products are simple, such as in the case of the conversion of methio-

Effects of Ozone *in vivo*

Comment	Reference
Higher sugar content increased susceptibility	*58*
	64
No effect in darkness	*65*
No effect on chlorophyll *a*. Inhibition of photosynthesis is log function of O_3 concentration	*66*
	14
Changes take place before visual symptoms	*67*
O_3 damage could be simulated by SH reagents	*68*
Initial inhibition of respiration eventually changes to stimulation. Mitochondria isolated from the latter tissue also showed increased O_2 uptake	*69*
Damage first observed in chloroplast stroma, similar to PAN damage	*70*
Greater loss of saturated rather than unsaturated fatty acids	*71*
Higher endogenous content of ascorbic acid did not protect	*72*
Injury developed 18 hrs later	*73*
Malonaldehyde detectable only after injury symptoms developed	*74*
	75
Chloroplast polysomes more susceptible than cytoplasmic	*76*
Chloroplast ribosomes more sensitive than cytoplasmic	*77*
Maximum susceptibility when soluble sugars and free amino acids are at minimum	*78*
After short ozone exposures photosynthesis recovers, and no damage becomes apparent	*79*

nine to methionine sulfoxide; in other cases, such as with tryptophan, however, there are many different products. These results have important implications for potential inactivation of proteins. There have been several reports of the reaction of ozone with reduced nicotinamides (51, 56, 57), and there is some difference of opinion as to the oxidation product. Menzel reports that it is the biologically active form (56), but our results indicate that the nicotinamide ring is opened (51).

Localization of double bonds in unknown compounds has frequently been determined by ozonolysis. Unsaturated fatty acids of biological membranes are susceptible to ozone attack, but there are some important differences from autoxidation reactions. These include the fact that malonaldehyde is produced from linoleate by ozonolysis (53) but not autoxidation and also that ozonolysis does not cause double bond conjugation as judged by absorption at 233 nm (52). Reactions with the polyunsaturated fatty acids produce several possibilities for toxic reactions: direct disruption of membrane integrity and toxic reactions caused by fatty acid hydroperoxides, hydrogen peroxide, and malonaldehyde.

Experiments in vitro are consistent with some of the chemical investigations. Enzymes are readily inactivated by ozone, and the inactivation can be traced to the more susceptible amino acid residues (Table XI). Reactions with unsaturated fatty acids have been examined, and the production of malonaldehyde and hydrogen peroxide has been detected (52–54). The lipid products have not been analyzed, and the toxicity of such products is yet to be determined.

Several reports of the effects of ozone in vivo are presented in Table XII. It is impossible to decide whether the effects of ozone are primary reactions or the result of a series of reactions initiated by ozone. All results can be rationalized as enzyme inhibition of one sort or another. Effects on membrane structure are harder to observe, and in one case it was reported that the malonaldehyde which would be expected on fatty acid ozonolysis was only observed after symptoms were apparent (74). Results of electron microscope examination showed that the first observable damage was in the stroma of the chloroplasts (70). One can easily argue that earlier damage could not be detected by microscopic techniques. However, recent reports that the chloroplast polyribosomes are much more susceptible to degradation by ozone are important observations which are consistent with the microscopy experiments (76). Chloroplast polysomes are also more susceptible to sulfhydryl reagents than are cytoplasmic polysomes (77). This evidence indicates that ozone itself, or a toxic product from primary oxidation, can pass through the cytoplasm and have its effect in the chloroplast.

There has been some interest in the effects of ozone on the amino acid metabolism of leaves. Tomlinson and Rich (67) reported an increase in γ-aminobutyric acid before visible symptoms were found. Ting and Mukerji (*78*) observed that the period of maximum susceptibility of cotton occurs when the soluble amino acids are at a minimum. Perhaps amino acids or other soluble components act as antioxidants and protect more sensitive components such as lipids or proteins. As far as the lipids are concerned, one might have expected the greatest effect on unsaturated fatty acids. In experiments with tobacco, this was not the case since the greatest reduction was in palmitic acid (*71*).

Conclusion

Considering the amount of research published on the effects of the four plant pollutants considered here, it is discouraging and perhaps embarrassing that we cannot describe in detail the sequence of events leading to the characteristic symptoms. Perhaps we should .simply cure the symptoms by using appropriate chemicals (*80, 81*) or use varieties of plants resistant to the pollutants (*2, 82*). One would like to believe that such considerations will be made redundant by lowering pollution to nontoxic levels.

Literature Cited

1. Jacobson, J. S., Hill, A. C., Eds., "Recognition of Air Pollution Injury to Vegetation," Air Pollution Control Association, Pittsburgh, Pa., 1970.
2. Menser, H. A., Heggestad, H. E., *Science* (1966) **153**, 424.
3. Dugger, W. M., Taylor, O. C., Cardiff, E. A., Thompson, C. R., *Proc. Amer. Soc. Hort. Sci.* (1962) **81**, 304.
4. Yang, S. F., *Biochemistry* (1970) **9**, 5008.
5. Shapiro, R., Servis, R. E., Welcher, M., *J. Amer. Chem. Soc.* (1970) **92**, 422.
6. Stevens, D. J., *J. Sci. Food Agr.* (1966) **17**, 202.
7. MacLeod, R. M., Farkas, W., Fridovitch, I., Handler, P., *J. Biol. Chem.* (1961) **236**, 1841.
8. Asada, K., Tamura, G., Bandurski, R. S., *J. Biol. Chem.* (1969) **244**, 4904.
9. Boyer, P. D., in "The Enzymes," Vol. 1, p. 511, 1959.
10. Hayatsu, H., Miura, A., *Biochem. Biophys. Res. Commun.* (1970) **39**, 156.
11. Mukai, F., Hawryuk, I., Shapiro, R., *Biochem. Biophys. Res. Commun.* (1970) **39**, 983.
12. LeBlanc, F., in "Air Pollution," p. 211, Centre for Agricultural Publishing and Documentation, Wageningen, 1969.
13. Syratt, W. J., Wanstall, P. J., Ref. *12*, p. 79.
14. de Koning, H. W., Jegier, Z., *Atmos. Environ.* (1968) **2**, 321.
15. Guderian, R., *Zeit, Pflanzenkrank, Pflanzenschutz* (1970) **77**, 200.
16. de Cormis, L., in Ref. *12*, p. 75.
17. Gilbert, O. L., in Ref. *12*, p. 223.
18. Jolly, W. L., "The Inorganic Chemistry of Nitrogen," Benjamin, New York, 1964.
19. Litchfield, C., Harlow, R. D., Isbell, A. F., Reiser, R., *J. Amer. Oil Chem. Soc.* (1965) **42**, 73.
20. Estefan, R. M., Gause, E. M., Rowlands, J. R., *Environ. Res.* (1970) **3**, 62.
21. Hudson, A., *Aust. J. Chem.* (1966) **19**, 1971.
22. Lijinsky, W., Epstein, S. S., *Nature (London)* (1970) **225**, 21.

23. Felmeister, A., Amanat, M., Weiner, N. D., *Environ. Sci. Technol.* (1968) **2**, 40.
24. Wray, J. L., Filner, P., *Biochem. J.* (1970) **119**, 715.
35. Mudd, J. B., Leavitt, R., Kersey, W. H., *J. Biol. Chem.* (1966) **241**, 4081.
26. Hill, A. C., Bennett, J. H., *Atmos. Environ.* (1970) **4**, 341.
27. Yung, K.-H., Mudd, J. B., *Plant Physiol.* (1966) **41**, 506.
28. Taylor, O. C., Eaton, F. M., *Plant Physiol.* (1966) **41**, 132.
29. Felmeister, A., Amanat, M., Weiner, N. D., *Atmos. Environ.* (1970) **4**, 311.
30. Kamel, A. M., Weiner, N. D., Felmeister, A., *Chem. Phys. Lipids* (1971) **6**, 225.
31. Mudd, J. B., Dugger, W. M., *Arch. Biochem. Biophys.* (1963) **102**, 52.
32. Stephens, E. R., *Atmos. Environ.* (1967) **1**, 19.
33. Mudd, J. B., *Arch. Biochem. Biophys.* (1963) **102**, 59.
34. Mudd, J. B., *J. Biol. Chem.* (1966) **241**, 4077.
35. Mudd, J. ., Leavitt, R., Kersey, W. H., *J. Biol. Chem.* (1966) **241**, 4081.
36. Mudd, J. B., McManus, T. T., *Arch. Biochem. Biophys.* (1969) **132**, 237.
37. Peak, M. J., Belser, W. L., *Atmos. Environ.* (1969) **3**, 385.
38. Ordin, L., Hall, M. A., *Plant Physiol.* (1967) **42**, 205.
39. Ordin, L., Propst, B., *Botan. Gaz.* (1962) **123**, 170.
40. Ordin, L., Hall, M. A., Katz, M., *J. Air Pollut. Control Assoc.* (1967) **17**, 811.
41. Darnall, K. R., Pitts, J. N., *Chem. Commun.* (1970) 1305.
42. Hall, M. A., Ordin, L., *Physiol. Plant* (1967) **20**, 624.
43. Thomson, W. W., Dugger, W. M., Palmer, R. L., *Bot. Gaz.* (1965) **126**, 66.
44. Taylor, O. C., *J. Air Pollut. Control Assoc.* (1969) **19**, 347.
45. Dugger, W. M., Ting, I. P., *Phytopathology* (1968) **58**, 8.
46. Gross, R. E., Dugger, W. M., *Environ. Res.* (1969) **2**, 256.
47. R. F. Gould, Ed., ADVAN. CHEM. SER. (1968) **77**.
48. ADVAN. CHEM. SER. (1959) **21**.
49. Bailey, P. S., *Chem. Rev.* (1958) **58**, 925.
50. Mudd, J. B., Leavitt, R., Ongun, A., McManus, T. T., *Atmos. Environ.* (1967) **3**, 669.
51. Mudd, J. B., *Arch. Environ. Health* (1965) **10**, 201.
52. Roehm, J. N., Hadley, J. G., Menzel, D. B., *Arch. Environ. Health* (1971) **23**, 142.
53. Mudd, J. B., McManus, T. T., Ongun, A., *Proc. 2nd Int. Clean Air Congr.* (1971) 256.
54. Baker, N., Wilson, L., *Biochem. Biophys. Res. Commun.* (1963) **11**, 6.
55. Mudd, J. B., McManus, T. T., Ongun, A., McCullogh, T. E., *Plant Physiol.* (1971) **48**, 335.
56. Menzel, D. B., *Arch. Environ. Health* (1971) **23**, 149.
57. Nasr, A. N. M., Dinman, B. D., Bernstein, I. A., *Arch. Environ. Health* (1971) **22**, 545.
58. Lee, T. T., *Can. J. Bot.* (1965) **43**, 677.
59. Freebain, H. T., *Science* (1957) **126**, 303.
60. Previero, A., Coletti-Previero, M. A., Jolles, P., *J. Mol. Biol.* (1967) **24**, 261.
61. Todd, G. W., *Physiol. Plant.* (1958) **11**, 457.
62. Ordin, L., Altman, A., *Physiol. Plant.* (1965) **18**, 790.
63. P'an, A. Y. S., Jegier, Z., *Arch. Environ. Health* (1970) **21**, 498.
64. Hanson, G. P., Stewart, W. S., *Science* (1970) **168**, 1223.
65. de Koning, H. W., Jegier, Z., *Arch. Environ. Health* (1969) **18**, 913.
66. de Koning, H. W., Jegier, Z., *Atmos. Environ.* (1968) **2**, 615.
67. Tomlinson, H., Rich, S., *Phytopathology* (1968) **57**, 808.
68. Tomlinson, H., Rich, S., *Phytopathology* (1968) **58**, 808.
69. Macdowall, F. D. H., *Can. J. Bot.* (1965) **43**, 419.
70. Thomson, W. W., Dugger, W. M., Palmer, R. L., *Can. J. Bot.* (1966) **44**, 1677.

71. Tomlinson, H., Rich, S., *Phytopathology* (1969) **59**, 1284.
72. Miller, P. R., Parmeter, J. R., Flick, B. H., Martinez, C. W., J. *Air Pollut. Control Assoc.* A1969) **19**, 435.
73. Tomlinson, H., Rich, S., *Phytopathology* (1970) **60**, 1842.
74. Tomlinson, H., Rich, S., *Phytopathology* (1970) **60**, 1531.
75. Tomlinson, H., Rich, S., *Phytopathology* (1971) **61**, 132.
76. Chang, C. W., *Phytochemistry* (1971) **10**, 2863.
77. Chang, C. W., *Biochem. Biophys. Res. Commun.* (1971) **44**, 1429.
78. Ting, I. P., Mukerji, S. K., *Amer. J. Bot.* (1971) **58**, 497.
79. Hill, A. C., Littlefield, N., *Environ. Sci. Technol.* (1969) **3**, 52.
80. Rich, S., Taylor, G. S., *Science* (1960) **132**, 150.
81. Freebain, H. T., Taylor, O. C., *Proc. Amer. Soc. Hort. Sci.* (1960) **76**, 693.
82. Hanson, G. P., Thorne, L., Jativa, C. D., *Proc. 2nd Int. Clean Air Congr.* (1971) 261.

RECEIVED April 7, 1972. Research supported by funds from the Environmental Protection Agency, Grant No. 800648 (formerly No. AP 00071).

5

Summary and Synthesis of Plant Toxicology

D. C. McCUNE

Boyce Thompson Institute for Plant Research, Yonkers, N. Y. 10701

Generally, the effects of air pollution on agriculture can be viewed as decreases in the value of a crop or increases in the cost of its production. One explains or predicts these effects by (a) experimentally determining what changes occur in the plant, its organs, or its cells with exposure to a pollutant under certain conditions; (b) collating this information, with respect to biological organization, changes in the pollutant, and the effects of environmental factors to describe the response of the plant; and (c) interpreting these changes in the plant's development or interaction with its environment with respect to social and economic values of a crop.

Reviews of air pollution are similar to pictures in some respects. Projections or perspectives differ, distorting some portions while revealing more accurately the relationships of others. Scales vary in order to present more detail but less scope for some areas of greater interest. Some types of features are depicted while others are ignored because the information must serve a particular need. Consequently, reviews may be almost as diverse as their subject. Moreover, our understanding of the effects of pollutants on plants is incomplete, and a picture of it cannot be drawn from some model as a whole. Instead, it must be assembled out of the jigsaw pieces of diverse and fragmentary knowledge. To summarize and synthesize the toxicology of air pollutants in plants is to sort out the segments of information, join them by inference, and fill in the gaps with speculation.

Form of Information

For more than a century scientists have investigated the action of air pollutants on vegetation. Although the results of this research are diverse, they can usually be reduced to simple statements exemplified by, "when this plant was exposed to this pollutant under these experimental conditions, the following effect was observed." Thus a primary unit of information contains four basic elements: receptor, pollutant, event, and environment. A definition of them and description of their properties, as they have appeared in the literature, are the starting points for this summary.

Receptor. A definition of receptor has three parts. First, a receptor is an object that may receive a pollutant and upon which observations are made. Secondly, although the term is singular, a receptor is a population of objects because experiments and inferences are usually based upon more than one individual. Thirdly, it is an entity at some point along the scale of biological organization.

By this definition the leaf is a typical receptor and one that has been studied frequently, but there are many kinds of receptors because more than one level of biological organization has been investigated. For example, plants, communities, and ecosystems have been observed in the field; tissues, cells, and cellular organelles have been taken from experimentally fumigated plants or studied *in situ;* and enzymes, mitochondria, and chloroplasts have been prepared and exposed to pollutants *in vitro.* There are other ways to categorize receptors besides level of biological organization. Genetic background is one. A receptor can be identified by its species, variety, or genotype when it is a plant or one of its components. A receptor can also be categorized by its function, structure, or position. For example, an enzyme can be identified by its activity, a cell by its morphology, and a plant by its place in a community.

Definitions and categories, however, usually are not air-tight, and sometimes it is difficult to decide what constitutes the receptor in a particular experiment. Is it the plant, leaf, or chloroplast if a group of plants is fumigated, leaves are harvested, and preparations of chloroplasts are tested for photosynthetic activity? If all leaves are taken, it could be the plant. If certain leaves are selected from each plant, it could be the leaf. If the chloroplasts are carefully prepared and fractionated, it could be the chloroplast of the mesophyll cell. The identity of a receptor is determined in many experiments not only by the methods that are used but also by the hypothesis that is tested.

Pollutant. A pollutant can be defined as a substance that is brought near a receptor by the atmosphere. A particular pollutant is distinguished from others by its physical and chemical properties. For example, it may be a gas or it may be an aerosol with a certain distribution of particle sizes; oxides of sulfur may be present as SO_2, SO_3, or H_2SO_4. The pollutant can also be characterized with respect to concentration, the length of time that a certain concentration is present, or the frequency distributions of periods of known duration and concentration (*1*). The pollutant could also be a mixture of two or more substances, and combinations of pollutants have been used in experimental fumigations more frequently in recent years.

Although it is easy to designate the pollutant in a controlled fumigation, it is more difficult to describe it when observations are made in the field. One reason is that the pollutant may actually be a group of substances of unknown composition, or the doses to which the receptor is exposed may be variable or unknown. Even if the source and its emissions are known, atmospheric processes not only transport but also transform emissions into pollutants. The atmospheric sorting of particulate materials, sorption of gases on particles, and the photochemical formation of smog in the Los Angeles area (2) are examples of this transformation. This is one reason why it is useful to distinguish between emissions at the source and pollutants near the receptor (the term "immission" has been used in Germany with reference to the receptor, but it is not used in the United States). Thus, when we come to field observations from experimental fumigations we may have to substitute "pollution from a particular source" for "pollutant," whether the latter is a single substance or a mixture.

Event. An event is a change in the character of the receptor. It is determined by an observational system according to some scale of measurement and at a time after exposure to the pollutant occurs. By this definition, there are many kinds of events, and attempts to categorize them have been based upon the kinds of receptors and observational systems (3, 4).

The activities of many enzymes are affected by fluorides (5) or by ozone (O_3) and peroxyacetyl nitrate (PAN) (6). Cells and their constituents, such as mitochondria, chloroplasts, or cell membranes, are structurally or functionally abnormal after exposure to many pollutants (7, 8, 9). With leaves, the most commonly reported event is the appearance of lesions (10, 11, 12), but altered gaseous exchange (13) and levels of metabolites (14) have also been found. Many of the events associated with plants can be classified as a change in their size or shape or as an accumulation of a pollutant when it is fluoride (15) or a metal (16, 17).

This definition of an event implies more than what may be illustrated by these examples; it is partially determined by the observational system, and it may comprise observations on more than one variate. For example, several characteristics of leaves which have been exposed to a pollutant may be determined by one means or another, and the non-fumigated and fumigated leaves may be represented by points in a space. The event, as it is defined, could be the distance between these two points, but because the receptor is defined as a population, variances and covariances as well as means should be considered and the points should be replaced by ellipsoids. Consequently, an event is a significant difference in one or more of the statistics that characterize the sample and is represented by a difference in the position, size, shape, or orientation of ellipsoids in a space whose dimensions are no greater than the number of variates or observational systems used.

Environment. The "environment" is a popular term and consequently has many meanings. It was chosen here for convenience and to designate conditions in an experiment. It can also be defined as the aggregate of all the external conditions and influences affecting the receptor, whether one knows all of these conditions, is able to decide which are more important, or measures and controls only the most significant of them. With respect to the plant, these environmental factors can be placed in broad categories, such as climatic or edaphic, if they act on the plant in the atmosphere or soil. Within these categories they can be classified according to their biological, chemical, or physical nature. Although many environmental factors are known to affect the plant, fewer are known to alter the plant's response to pollutants. Among the latter are climatic factors (temperature, relative humidity, light intensity and quality, photoperiod) and edaphic factors (availability of mineral nutrients, soil temperature and moisture tension). The presence of pathogenic organisms or insects, in the soil or air, are also environmental factors whose significance in air pollution is becoming better known. When mixtures of pollutants are used in a factorial experiment, one could regard the presence of one or more pollutants as environmental factors that modify the effect of another pollutant.

Just as there are different kinds of receptors, there are different kinds of environments. For example, the environment of an enzyme is an aqueous solution in which pH, ionic strength, temperature, and concentrations of cofactors or substrates are significant. At every level, the environment is variable because conditions can change rapidly with time, and it is complex because a number of factors are present, and one factor seldom varies independently from the others.

Patterns of Explanation

The model for experimental results, which has been developing, reduces and sorts various information into manageable portions, but it only hints at the way in which these pieces fit together. What must now be sought are patterns that can unite them into descriptions and explanations of the effects of air pollutants. There are many possible patterns, but those that suit the form of our information and embody the ideas of temporal and spatial order are probably the most useful. Thus, the characteristics of receptors, pollutants, events, and environments can be elaborated into patterns that could be called (a) hierarchy of biological organization, (b) course of the pollutant, (c) response of biological systems, and (d) environmental interactions.

Biological Organization. The leaf functions as a part of a plant and, together with other organs, constitutes the plant. Plants in turn reside in a community, contribute to its structure, and participate in its life. Each leaf also comprises a number of tissues, and its structure and function derive from their structural and functional organization. Similarly, tissues consist of cells, and structures of the cell consist of macromolecules, such as protein, lipid, or polysaccharide. From protein to community, biological organization establishes a hierarchical relationship between different kinds of receptors. Accordingly, when an event is observed, its causes are explained as the changes that have been produced previously in the receptor's components, and its consequences are predicted in terms of the altered role that the receptor may play in some larger system.

The patterns of chlorosis, pigmentation, or necrosis that appear on the leaf following exposure to a pollutant can be explained as the sum of changes in its individual cells—loss of chlorophyll, pigment formation, or death. A change in the foliar content of free amino acids or soluble sugars can be attributed to changes in the sizes of metabolite pools within the cells. If there is less functional photosynthetic tissue on the leaf because of necrosis or chlorosis or if there are reduced levels of metabolites, then lesser amounts of sugars may be formed and translocated to the rest of the plant and a smaller plant may result from this tighter photosynthetic budget. In these examples, the propagation of a change through a biological system is direct, and the changes observed in the plant or leaf are no greater than the aggregate of those occurring in its components. However, the more numerous hypotheses for the action of air pollutants involve a multiplicative instead of an additive mechanism. With the leaf this mechanism may operate where a change occurs in the relatively few cells that determine the flow of materials between leaf and plant or between leaf and environment. One example is the occurrence of tyloses in cells of petiolar vascular bundles in plants exposed to fluoride (18). Another is the effects of ozone and sulfur dioxide on the guard cells of the stomata; a diminished uptake of CO_2 could accompany the closure of the stomata (19), and an increased loss of water could result from increased stomatal apertures (20).

Other kinds of multiplicative mechanisms operate as a result of the structural and functional position of the receptor and event. Among the different macromolecules, attention has been focused on two kinds of receptors: protein and lipid. The first as enzymes, and both as constituents of membranes, mitochondria, chloroplasts, or other cellular organelles, have been studied *in vitro* with respect to pollutants, such as fluoride, PAN, or O_3. Inhibitions of enzyme activity by fluoride are usually attributed to the formation of a complex that blocks an active site. For example, the inhibition of enolase activity is attributed to the formation of fluoromagnesium phosphate at the catalytic site (5). On the other hand, the mechanism of action of an oxidant may involve possibilities such as a direct effect on the catalytic site, oxidation or acetylation of some cofactors, or disruption of the enzyme structure (6). In cellular organelles, structure and function are tightly bound, and both are changed by pollutants. There is no direct evidence as to what specific moiety is changed although the oxidation of amino acid residues of proteins and olefinic bonds of lipids have been suggested.

Because the enzyme functions as a catalyst, its inhibition or inactivation may decrease the rate of a particular metabolic reaction. The reduction in the rate of this reaction may inhibit the pathway in which this reaction occurs and, in turn, result in the depletion of a product or the accumulation of precursors or intermediates. Changes in O_2 or CO_2 exchange, pools of various metabolites, and the metabolism of glucose (both catabolism and incorporation into cell wall polysaccharides) that have been observed also support this hypothesis.

Similarly, a change in mitochondrion, chloroplast, or cell membrane disturbs respiration, photosynthesis, or accumulation of substances by the cell. Because of a lack of materials or energy to process them, the structural integrity of the cell suffers and fails. In histological studies cellular dysfunction usually appears as a loss of chlorophyll from the chloroplast and water in the intercellular spaces, and death of the cell appears as a general collapse and pigment formation although some intermediate stages may be seen (21).

Changes in the plant itself can be explained in a similar manner because of the types of events and their position in the system—*i.e.*, they affect the critical processes of transmission or transformation. Although many of these changes occur in the vegetative processes of the plant, the more significant ones would be those that affect its reproduction. Decreased assimilation by leaves or their premature senescence and abscission could impair formation of reproductive organs, fruit development, or the growth of storage organs (22, 23). Of course, the direct effect of the pollutant would be on the reproductive tissues themselves in the form of altered pollen germination (23), aberrant embryo development, or apparent mutagenesis (24).

Course of Pollutants. Basically the description of the action of air pollutants in plants has taken the same form as the aphorism, "for want of a nail, . . . the rider was lost," except that in environmental problems, there is also concern about the fate of a missing nail. Thus a chain of events that interprets changes in a pollutant as well as in a receptor is a necessary part of the mode of action of air pollutants.

A typical pollutant arrives at the plant after undergoing the atmospheric processes that can be considered as its generation or as the first of a series of transformations. Generally, pollutants act within a leaf or other organ and not at a distance from it. An exception to this may be the deposits of soot or dusts that form on the surface of a leaf or clog the stomata and thereby screen out light or impede gaseous exchange. However, the primary event in the course of a pollutant is its reaction in and with the aqueous medium that surrounds the cells after it penetrates the leaf through the epidermis or stomata. Within the aqueous phase, it may react with more than one chemical species, including water, because pollutants have a broad reactivity and many reactions can be postulated (6). The pollutant in a new form or one of the other products of a reaction may then affect the biological system. Also, the consumption of some compound by reaction with the pollutant rather than the production of a product may be a biologically significant event. The pollutant may then be transformed into salts or metabolites within the cells, distributed within the plant's tissues, and ultimately pass to the soil through exudation from roots, elution from leaves, or leaching from dead foliage and other plant debris. Although the pollutant can be defined as a particular substance in some part of the environment, its effects must be interpreted with respect to its course—*i.e.*, those changes it undergoes as it moves to the receptor, traverses the biological system, and meets its fate in some other portion of the environment.

Sulfur dioxide (SO_2) is a typical pollutant with respect to the preceding scheme. Within the aqueous phase of the leaf, it forms a hydrated complex (clathrate) and then sulfite or bisulfite ions. These ions may act as pollutants for a macromolecular receptor, but other reactions may occur and be important. Superoxide, bisulfite, or other radicals as well as hydrogen peroxide may be generated with the oxidation of sulfite to sulfate in the presence of ligated or free metals (25), and these products may be toxic. Other examples are the formation of coordination compounds with metals [*e.g.*, iron(III)] and the sulfonation of compounds having aldehydic, olefinic, or disulfide groups. Some of the compounds (NAD, thiamin, FAD, folate, and uracil) that react with bisulfite *in vitro* are cofactors of enzymes or constituents of them, but the importance of these reactions *in vivo* has not been demonstrated. After oxidation to sulfate, sulfur derived from SO_2 may supply up to 40% of the plant's requirement, and it can enter the sulfur pool, be converted to sulfur-containing metabolites, and then be rapidly translocated throughout the plant (13). There is also evidence that sulfur from SO_2

is reduced to hydrogen sulfide in the light and released to the atmosphere by the plant (*26*).

The course of the pollutant can be illustrated with other major pollutants. The oxidation of NADH or NADPH by PAN and O_3 could remove cofactors required in enzymatic activity. The oxidation of free amino acids could generate inhibitors of metabolic reactions. The complexing of metals (such as Ca, Mg, Cu, Zn, or Fe) by fluoride could sequester metabolically significant cations. Perhaps the formation of a fluoroferrate or fluoroaluminate complex is metabolically significant.

Although direct evidence is lacking, the nitrogen derived from oxides of nitrogen (NO_x) may also enter the nitrogen pool and be incorporated and translocated within the plant. However, the accumulation and metabolism in the tissue of pollutants, which have longer lifetimes than the oxidants, may be as important as their reactions in solution. For example, fluoride, sulfate, or chloride is accumulated in the foliar tissues, and the plant may then pass it on to the soil or other organisms. Moreover, with pollutants not normally thought of as entering the metabolism of the receptor, metabolic transformation may also be important. For example, the biosynthesis of fluoroorganic compounds has been known for several genera in the Southern Hemisphere, but the hypothesis that some common crop plants also can incorporate a significant amount of inorganic fluoride into monofluoroacetate (*27*) has not been completely resolved.

Responses of Biological Systems. Although organization is one guide in the connection of receptors and events, the temporal development of biological systems is equally important because the character of the receptor changes with time. As a receptor originates from and participates in the life of some other entity, it goes through the progressive and periodic changes that constitute its life cycle. With perennials, such as a tree, there are cyclic, seasonal changes superimposed on a life cycle of much longer duration. With a leaf, the diurnal changes may be much less apparent than those occurring as it unfolds, matures, and then yellows and drops. With an enzyme the major changes may be cyclical as it goes from one state to another during the reaction it catalyzes. The composite of these changes could be described as a line, which may be discontinuous, that connects the points in some space defined by observational systems. Perhaps a blurred line should be used because of variation seen in a population. Therefore, one can have a series of events if exposure to a pollutant or observations are continued over a period of time; one path will be followed by the treated receptor while another is followed by the control. This series of events or divergence in paths could be called the response of a receptor to a pollutant.

A number of terms can be used to describe the characteristics of a response; threshold is one. One can expose a plant to a pollutant and find that a certain response does not occur when the concentration of the pollutant is equal to or less than some value. Thresholds have been found experimentally for the major pollutants, mainly with respect to foliar lesions, and most explanations of thresholds involve mechanisms concerned with the probability that the pollutant will reach a particular receptor, that an event will be produced, or that an event will be propagated through the system.

At the molecular level, the buffering capacity of the cellular solution may block the pollutant in its course. Pollutants that generate acids or bases may be neutralized by acid–base buffers. Excess calcium or other cations may complex fluoride, and redox systems may buffer SO_2, O_3, or PAN, or the free radicals they generate. On another level, enzyme structure determines whether the pollutant will penetrate and react with an active site, and the functioning of an enzyme, apparently through effects on its structure, also modifies its susceptibility to the pollutant (6). Moreover, inhibition of a susceptible enzyme may not affect a pathway: the enzyme affected may not be rate-limiting in a particular pathway, and considerably greater inhibition must occur before it is.

One can expect the same types of mechanisms, which can operate at other levels, to explain thresholds and their variability. The numbers and condition of the stomata will determine how much of the pollutant will reach the mesophyll cells of the leaf. Indeed, the "reflex-type resistance" (4) of the plant is attributed to the closure of stomata in response to O_3, which thereby impedes further entrance of these pollutants. Young or old tobacco leaves are very resistant to oxidants. When young, a leaf's resistance may be attributed to the density of the cells, which limits penetration of gases into the mesophyll. In the mature and aging leaf, suberization of the cell walls blocks the penetration of the pollutants (28). The cells of the leaf and their susceptibility to oxidants illustrate another aspect of the threshold and response—they are determined by the stage of development of the receptor, and different mechanisms operate at different times.

Another characteristic of the response is attenuation. That is, the magnitude of the response may decrease with time. The threshold and attenuation of a response would appear to be related mechanistically because both could involve homeostatic processes in a receptor and regenerative or compensatory mechanisms. Although the capacity of buffering systems may account for a threshold, their metabolic regeneration, through the reduction of sulfhydryl groups or translocation of cations, may account for attenuation. The metabolic changes found are probably the result of a shift to an alternate pathway as well as the inhibition of a particular one. For example, one explanation for the changes seen in glucose catabolism after tissue has been treated with fluoride is an inhibition of glycolysis and a shift to pentose phosphate metabolism. There are also possibilities of feedback mechanisms in which the depletion of a product releases end-product inhibition and precursor accumulation leads to enzyme induction. At the level of the cell, repair of the cell membrane after an initial disruption of its integrity by oxidants may account for apparent recovery.

Even where acute changes drastically alter the plant, regeneration and compensation are evident. The reduction in photosynthetically functional surface is compensated by the presence of unaffected leaves that are lower in the canopy and that now receive more light (4). On the other hand, regeneration rather than compensation may occur after exposure to the pollutant has ceased by the release of axillary buds or continued growth of the shoots that replace the lost foliar tissue.

While there is a threshold for one kind of response, another kind of response may occur at another level of organization, and this point has been discussed with respect to air pollution (29). Similarly, the attenuation of one response may not be accompanied by the attenuation of another, and more evidence is needed for this point. It could also be argued that one may see only an apparent threshold because a response would have been seen if some later time had been chosen for observation. This is a valid point because in addition to a threshold there may be a latency in a response, and the time-course is an important aspect of a response. Latency could be attributed to the amount of time required for the propagation or expression of an event; time must pass before a change in flower or leaf is manifest as a change in fruit. However, for fluorides, perhaps for chlorides, sulfates, and metals, the latent period may reflect the length of time required for pollutants, which are absorbed over the entire organ, to be translocated and concentrated in the tissues that respond. There is also the possibility that the time lag in the propagation of a change may account for the amplification of a response. For example, the initial lesions produced in a leaf may be followed by premature senescence and abscission, which remove the entire leaf. The loss of this tissue could then lead to decreased growth of other portions of the plant. The result, whether by lesions, abscission, or decreased growth, is a much reduced foliar mass than originally observed. Amplification may also occur where changes in one cell sensitize its neighbors to a pollutant; the analysis of dose–response curves (relating pattern of injury to dose of oxidant) might reveal a contagious distribution of lesions.

Generally, there are two important aspects to a biological process— function and control. For the most part, the toxic effects of air pollutants have been interpreted in terms of an inhibition of function rather than a loss of control. Experiments with fluoride salts or oxidants *in vitro* have dealt with effects on enzyme activity, but there are few experimental data as to the effects of these pollutants on the allosteric or regulatory sites of enzymes. To a lesser extent the same is true of responses at the cellular level. However, two fairly common responses are associated with leaves and suggest that this type of amplification mechanism may operate. One is the abscission of leaves, which is known to be under hormonal control. The other is the savoying effect, often seen in developing leaves that have been exposed to pollutants, where growth of laminar tissue is not in its normal relationship to that of vascular tissues. Perhaps a third would be the smaller leaves and more twiggy growth of plants exposed to HF (*30*). Experiments with isolated tissues show that some interaction occurs between pollutants and plant growth substances. The effects of pollutants on the formation, translocation, or action of auxins, gibberellins, cytokinins, abscissic acid, or ethylene, certainly deserve further investigation.

   Environmental Interactions. The characteristics of the receptor's response may be explained in terms of access of the pollutant to portions of a biological system and other mechanisms that involve positive and negative feedback in the propagation of an event. However, the operations of these mechanisms vary with a receptor's development, and the phenotype of the receptor and its development depend on environmental conditions as well as on its genetic complement. One of the best illustrations of the complex nature of the interaction of genes and environment in determining the response of a plant to air pollutants is found with oxidants and tobacco (*31*). Thus the environment before, during, and after a receptor's exposure to a pollutant must be considered a determining factor in shaping the biological system, the course of the pollutant, and the response.

   Changes in environmental conditions alter the plant's response to a pollutant in several ways (*22, 32*). One of the best examples of an environmental factor operating at different levels and by different mechanisms is the effect of light on oxidant-induced effects. A light period of about four hours is required before, during, and after exposure to PAN for foliar lesions to occur. This effect may be partially caused by a closing of stomata in darkness, which reduces the access of PAN to the interior of the leaf. This mechanism would also explain why less fluoride is accumulated and the resistance of leaves to lesions induced by SO_2 or Cl_2 is greater in darkness. It would also explain why foliar water stress, induced by soil water deficit or by low relative humidity (edaphic or climatic factors), reduces HF- or SO_2-induced foliar lesions through stomatal closure. However, light may induce other mechanisms of action.

For example, the photosynthetic system may be the primary site of action, and photosynthesis or at least photochemical activity is necessary for sensitization or for the effects of PAN to be amplified. Similarly, the length of the dark period preceding exposure to light and O_3 determines the occurrence and degree of the metabolic and foliar effects observed (9). For ozone, sugar metabolism may be important in making the affected site one that is rate limiting or more susceptible to attack. On the other hand, light-induced reactions could inhibit the metabolic processes that repair PAN-induced injury (9, 33).

Another kind of environmental interaction may result when in a homeostatic adjustment to the pollutant, the plant sacrifices part of its capacity to respond to environmental fluctuations. For example, the metabolic adjustment to fluorides may increase the susceptibility to nutrient stress. This hypothesis could explain why some symptoms of chronic fluoride toxicity resemble those produced by Mn, Fe, or Zn deficiencies. If air pollution is one environmental factor that alters the susceptibility of the plant to other environmental stress, it would also be logical to expect an interaction between pollutants if the receptor is exposed to two or more of them. Such interactive effects have been found. Sub-threshold concentrations of SO_2 and O_3 or SO_2 and NO_2 produce foliar lesions when plants are exposed to both pollutants (34). Additionally, plants exposed to SO_2 differ from non-fumigated plants in their resistance to subsequent fumigations (35). Thus the plant's susceptibility or capacity to adapt to a pollutant is altered by concurrent exposures to another or consecutive exposures to the same one.

There is also the possibility that pollutants alter susceptibility of the plant to pathogens (36) or insect attack. Of the latter there is the decreased resistance of ponderosa pine to bark beetle attack caused by ambient oxidant exposure (37). The investigations of others with respect to the effects of fluoride on ponderosa pine indicated that although foliar injury was associated with increased resin exudation pressure, which could be interpreted as an increased capacity of the tree to overcome bark beetle attack, degree of insect infestation was not associated with amount of foliar injury (38). As more is known about pheromones, the botanical investigation of the secondary products of metabolism, such as terpenes and phenolics, may become more important in investigating the mode of action of pollutants in the entire plant. The switch to alternate pathways, while resulting in the same products, may reduce the intermediates needed in biosynthesis and thereby affect the plant's resistance to disease or attractiveness to insects.

A plant's relationship to its environment is often envisaged as that of the cow's in Stevenson's verse, "and blown by all the winds that pass/And wet with all the showers." However, the plant's role is not completely passive. It interacts with its environment and modifies it, and so does every receptor whether it is an enzyme, cell, or organism. It is through this interaction of receptor and environment that the latter is not only an ambient milieu but also a channel for information and part of the organization of a biological system. Possibly, one result of the response of plants to air pollutants is an altered environment. For example, a consequence of an effect of pollutants on stomata could be a change in soil moisture tension.

By nature of biological organization, the internal state of one receptor becomes the environment of another. Although some environmental conditions, such as temperature, are rapidly communicated from one level to another, others will be modified in degree and type as they filter down through sucecssive layers. Mineral nutrition of the plant may ultimately affect the aqueous environment of enzyme or cell and thereby alter its susceptibility to pollutants. For example, calcium stress induces susceptibility of the plant to HF with respect to effects on fruit development, but whether these effects are the result of prevention or amelioration of a response is not known. At each level one can postulate that the environment acts by affecting the course of the pollutant, partially determining the character and development of the receptor, and modifying the response of a receptor to a pollutant. These changes are reciprocal, however, and, in effect, one can speak of the receptor's response to the pollutant in broader terms. Its response is really a change in its interaction with its environment.

The Agricultural Picture

Because the effect of air pollution on agriculture is the unifying theme of this volume, the following question might be raised: "To what extent or in what way do these hypothetical models explain it?" The answer is that the same general models and hypothetical mechanisms that have been used to interpret experimental data can also be used for effects on agriculture if a new reference system is used. Two have been proposed—one for agriculture effects (39) and another expanded system for effects on forests and recreational areas (40)—to simplify and transform biological effects to economic and social consequences. One can simplify receptors by excluding receptors that are not agriculturally significant, and one can also simplify effects of air pollution, but the two aspects of the development of the receptor and its response to the pollutant are important: end-point and pathway.

The response of the plant, or some other receptor, to the pollutant has been judged mainly with reference to its normal course of development, but in agriculture the end of the course of development may not be a natural one; the fate of the spinach leaf is not senescence and death but the dinner table in an appetizing condition. Accordingly, foliar lesions are more important with respect to the plant's saleability than its reproductive capacity. Thus, those direct effects that are exemplified by a decreased quantity or quality of a product reflect a pollutant-induced change in the end point.

Because the end point is known beforehand, the pathway is probably as important as the destination, and a certain end point may be reached by more than one path. Ideally, one tries to set the plant's biological program (plant breeding) and manipulate its environment (cultivation) to achieve an end point of greatest probable yield by a pathway of least possible work. The indirect effects of pollutants on agriculture are therefore a reflection of the fact that the response to pollution represents a less efficient path or that additional work will be required to reach the same destination. For example, one will have to spray the spinach with an antioxidant or breed smog-resistant varieties.

Agriculture appears to be a specialized case of a community or ecosystem with a simpler system and more clearly defined values for judgment, and research into the effects of air pollutants upon it has a two-fold significance. First, the results of this research can be used to improve environmental quality with respect to present pollutants. Secondly, the methodology developed by this research can be used to evaluate, with greater efficiency, the environmental consequences of pollutants that may appear in the future.

To summarize toxicology of air pollutants in plants is to try to draw a map of a part of the real world with economic and social features placed over the natural ones. However, our map resembles one from an earlier era; the well-known or self-evident is shown correctly, but the frontiers are distorted or displaced from their true position, and much unknown territory is left blank awaiting future, scientific exploration.

Literature Cited

1. Wanta, R. C., in "Air Pollution," 2nd ed., Vol. 1, A. C. Stern, Ed., pp. 187–226, Academic, New York, 1968.
2. Schuck, E. A., ADVAN. CHEM. SER. (1973) **122,** 1.
3. Weinstein, L. H., McCune, D. C., *J. Air Pollut. Contr. Ass.* (1971) **21,** 410.
4. Vogl, M., Börtitz, S., Polster, H., *Biol. Zentralbl.* (1965) **84,** 763.
5. Wiseman, A., in "Handbook of Experimental Pharmacology," Vol. 20, Part 2, pp. 48–97, F. A. Smith, Ed., Springer Verlag, New York, 1970.
6. Mudd, J. B., ADVAN. CHEM. SER. (1973) **122,** 31.
7. Treshow, M., *Annu. Rev. Phytopath.* (1971) **9,** 21.
8. Rich, S., *Annu. Rev. Phytopath.* (1964) **2,** 253.
9. Dugger, W. M., Ting, I. P., *Annu. Rev. Plant Physiol.* (1970) **21,** 215.
10. Taylor, O. C., ADVAN. CHEM. SER. (1973) **122,** 9.

11. Hindawi, I. J., "Air Pollution Injury to Vegetation," National Air Pollution Control Administration, Raleigh, N. C., 1970.
12. Jacobson, J. S., Hill, A. C., Eds., "Recognition of Air Pollution Injury to Vegetation. A Pictorial Atlas," Air Pollution Control Association, Pittsburgh, 1970.
13. Thomas, M. D., in "Air Pollution," pp. 233–278, World Health Organization, Geneva, 1961.
14. McCune, D. C., Weinstein, L. H., MacLean, D. C., Jacobson, J. S., in "Agriculture and the Quality of Our Environment," N. C. Brady, Ed., pp. 33–44, AAAS, Washington, D. C., 1967.
15. National Research Council, Committee on Biologic Effects of Atmospheric Pollutants, "Fluorides," National Academy of Sciences, Washington, D. C., 1971.
16. Lagerwerff, J. V., in "Agriculture and the Quality of Our Environment," N. C. Brady, Ed., pp. 343–64, AAAS, Washington, D. C., 1967.
17. Berge, H., "Phytotoxische Immisionen (Gas-, Rauch- und Staubschäden)," Verlag Paul Parey, Berlin, 1963.
18. Poovaiah, B. W., Wiebe, H. H., Phytopathology (1969) 59, 518.
19. Gabelman, W. H., Hort. Sci. (1970) 5, 250.
20. Majernik, O., Mansfield, T. A., Phytopath. Z. (1971) 71, 123.
21. Darley, E. F., Middleton, J. T., Annu. Rev. Phytopath. (1966) 4, 103.
22. van Haut, H., Stratmann, H., "Color-Plate Atlas of the Effects of Sulfur Dioxide on Plants," Verlag W. Giradet, Essen, 1970.
23. Feder, W. A., ADVAN. CHEM. SER. (1973) 122, 21.
24. Mohammed, A. H., J. Air Pollut. Control Ass. (1968) 18, 395.
25. McCord, J. M., Fridovich, I., J. Biol. Chem. (1969) 244, 6056.
26. de Cormis, L., Proc. European Congr. Influence Air Pollut. Plants Animals, 1st, Wageningen, 1969, pp. 75–78.
27. Cheng, J. Y.-O., Yu, M.-H., Miller, G. W., Welkie, G. W., Environ. Sci. Technol. (1968) 2, 367.
28. Glater, R. B., Solberg, R. A., Scott, F. M., Amer. J. Bot. (1962) 49, 954.
29. Dinman, B. D., Science (1972) 175, 495.

RECEIVED May 25, 1972. Project financed partly with federal funds from the Environmental Protection Agency, grant R-801070. Contents do not necessarily reflect the views and policies of EPA. Use of tradenames or commercial products does not constitute endorsement.

6

Colonizing Genetic Populations as Units of Regulated Change

JAMES HARDING

Department of Environmental Horticulture, University of California, Davis, Calif. 95616

Variation at four genetic loci was found in 29 populations of Lupinus succulentus *from throughout California. A mathematical model was developed, and estimators were derived for the parameters, gene frequency, heterozygote frequency, rate of cross-fertilization, and coefficient of inbreeding. Estimates indicate that (1) variation is nearly always present for the S/s locus affecting seed pigmentation, (2) variation is generally but not always absent for the loci, B/b, P/p, and D/d, affecting flower pigmentation, (3) variation is not reduced in populations from recently colonized sites, (4) rates of cross-fertilization range from zero to nearly 100% with a mean near 0.50, and (5) coefficients of inbreeding vary from zero to 0.80 with a mean near 0.40. The results do not suggest that man's disturbance of the environment has had any deleterious effect on the genetic structure of* Lupinus succulentus, *but this species was chosen for study because it has been a successful colonizer.*

The genetic structure of a population at any point in time can be expressed as a function of directed and nondirected forces. The directed forces include natural selection, mutation, migration, and inbreeding. Genetic drift, on the other hand, causes genetic populations to vary in a nondirected random manner. These processes all exert a measure of regulation on a genetic population. Genetic structure for the simple case of a single genetic locus with alleles A and a can be described by:

D = frequency of homozygous AA, H = frequency of heterozygous Aa, and R = frequency of homozygous aa.

If mating is random, these genotypic frequencies are functions of p, the frequency of the allele A, and q, the frequency of the allele a, *viz.*

$$D = p^2$$
$$H = 2pq \tag{1}$$
$$R = q^2$$

where $q = R + H/2$ and $p + q = 1$. This assumes there is no selection, there is no mutation or migration, and the population is infinitely large, *i.e.*, no genetic drift.

Many species of plants reproduce, in part, by self-fertilization, and, therefore, Equation 1 apply only to individuals that result from cross-fertilization. The inbreeding which results from self-fertilization can be defined by the parameter F, the decrease in the frequency of heterozygotes (*1*), and Equation 1 becomes

$$D = p^2 + pqF$$
$$H = 2pq\ (1 - F) \tag{2}$$
$$R = q^2 + pqF$$

Such a population will approach equilibrium where $F = (1 - \alpha)/(1 + \alpha)$ (*2*). The parameter α defines the binomial frequency for cross-fertilization, and $(1 - \alpha)$ defines the frequency for self-fertilization. The population can now be described in terms of its reproductive mode (*3*)—*viz.*,

$$D = p(1 + \alpha - 2\alpha q)/(1 + \alpha)$$
$$H = 4pq\alpha/(1 + \alpha) \tag{3}$$
$$R = q(1 - \alpha + 2\alpha q)/(1 + \alpha)$$

If genes are migrating into this population and the frequency among immigrating genes, q_m, is not the same as q, then the structure of the population will be further altered. The populations can be partitioned into two fractions, the immigrants, m, and the natives, $1 - m$. The change in gene frequency from one generation to the next, Δq, is given by

$$\Delta q = (q_m - q)m \tag{4}$$

This can be substituted into Equation 3 to obtain expressions for changes in genotypic frequencies.

Genes are also subject to recurrent mutation. Gene A can mutate to gene a at a rate μ, and gene a can mutate to gene A at a rate v. The change in gene frequency caused by mutation rates is given by

$$\Delta q = \mu p - vq \tag{5}$$

Since mutation rates are generally less than 10^{-5} per generation (4), this effect is quite small over short time intervals.

In finite populations gene frequency will change from generation to generation because each generation represents a sample of the previous generation. The change in gene frequency that results from random sampling is called genetic drift. The magnitude of Δq is inversely proportional to population size, N. In any generation the dispersion in q is given by the variance in Δq, viz.

$$\sigma^2_q(F = 0) = \frac{pq}{2N} \tag{6}$$

where $2N$ is the number of genes in the random mating diploid population (5). If the population is totally inbred, i.e., $F = 1$, then there are only N genes free to vary, and Equation 6 becomes

$$\sigma 1^2_{\Delta q}(F = 1) = \frac{pq}{N} \tag{7}$$

Consequently, the more highly self-fertilizing the population, the larger are the dispersive effects of genetic drift.

Expectations for the genotypic frequencies D, H, and R can be formulated in terms of inbreeding (F), migration rate (m), mutation rates $(\mu$ and $v)$, and drift (q, N). The extent to which empirical estimates of D, H, and R deviate from these expectations has been taken as a measure of natural selection (3). Consequently, the magnitude of natural selection is deduced from our inability to explain genetic frequencies on other grounds. The survival rate or fitness value, W, of a genotype has been defined as the ratio of observed to expected frequency, placing the average fitness of the population, W, at unity (6). These fitnesses are given by

$$W_{AA} = D/E(D)$$
$$W_{Aa} = H/E(H) \tag{8}$$
$$W_{aa} = R/E(R)$$

Colonization

It seems likely that the genetic structure of a population will be altered by different selective pressures encountered as a population colonizes a new habitat. Therefore, the processes responsible for genetic structure need to be reviewed within the context of colonization. By any evolutionary time standard colonization is short term and mutation rates are too low to have any appreciable effect on genetic structure. Similarly, gene migration is generally of lesser importance as a population colonizes a new habitat, often in a new area for the species. Remember that gene migration is not to be confused with dispersal. Thus gene migration and mutation are likely to be of negligible importance and hereafter are ignored.

Genetic drift, on the other hand, takes on considerable importance in colonization. Founder populations can be small and include a limited amount of genetic variability. This founder effect is a special case of genetic drift and appears to be of major significance in birds (7).

Colonization may also be associated with a change in the reproductive mode of a population. Baker (8) has suggested that dispersal over long distances will usually involve a single or few seeds. This is not likely to result in the establishment of a colony unless the individuals are capable of self-fertilization. This has led to the common observation that self-fertilization generally occurs around the periphery of a distribution. Baker's studies have been based on genus and species comparisons, but the tendency toward self-fertilization may be extended to the level of the genetic population. If so, the inbreeding coefficient F may be greatly increased in colonial populations. This would increase the genetic uniformity even beyond that suggested by Mayr's founder effect.

The role of natural selection in colonization has been considered by Stebbins (9). He suggests that colonizing populations fluctuate greatly in numbers, often becoming extinct. Reproductive potential must be high to recolonize new habitats continually. Part of the reproductive capacity of a colony is its ability to produce uniformly adapted offspring rather than segregating offspring with different adaptive properties. Consequently, selection, as well as the founder effect and the dispersal effect, is expected to increase genetic uniformity. If this hypothesis is true, then environmental disturbances that foster increased colonizations will have a negative effect on the conservation of genetic variability. This hypothesis is tested with the following materials and methods.

Experimental Material

Lupinus succulentus Dougl. (Fabaceae) is an annual California native which has become ruderal in many areas (10). Roadside populations are more numerous now than natural populations. The latter tend to occur in habitats with a considerable degree of disturbance, suggesting that this species may have been preadapted for colonization. Since road building is continuing, colonizing episodes are constantly initiated. In some cases, founders can be traced to their parental natural population. Some populations may be available for long-term studies, but most are transient and available for only a few years. Nevertheless, such populations offer unique opportunities to study genetic populations during the early stages of colonization.

The flowers of *Lupinus succulentus* are predominantly dark blue. Rarely, variants occur which are light blue, pink, or entirely white flowered. These are all conditioned by recessive alleles, *viz.*, *dd* for light blue, *pp* for pink, and *bb* for white. All three dominant genes, *D*, *P*, and *B*, are required for the expression of the dark blue color. The presence or absence of a band of dark pigmentation across the seed coat, Figure 1, was found to segregate in most populations; the recessive *ss* is bandless.

The greatest part of the geographic distribution of *Lupinus succulentus* is along the Pacific Coast of California. This *coastal* group is represented by many populations from Tehema County, Calif., to San Diego County, Calif. Populations occur in the foothills of the North

Figure 1.   Seed coat genotypes, ss for bandless and S- for banded

Coast, South Coast, Transverse, and Peninsular Ranges. Surveys of genotypic frequencies in natural and ruderal populations were made from samples taken from collection areas A through F (Figure 2) and G through P (Figure 3).

The surveys indicate that all populations sampled are phenotypically dominant for *B* and *P*. Most populations are *DD* or *Dd;* notable exceptions are the Lower Putah Populations, which have varying frequencies of *dd*. Pollinator preference for the dark blue flower color may account for the relatively infrequent occurrence of polymorphisms for loci affecting flower color. In contrast, the *S/s* locus is polymorphic in nearly all populations sampled (Tables I, II, and III), the exceptions being Mace-11, San Gregorio-1 (based on only 34 individuals, *i.e.*, 68 *s* alleles) and Mission Bay-1. Populations, therefore, are generally homozygous *BBPPDD* and polymorphic for the alleles *S* and *s*.

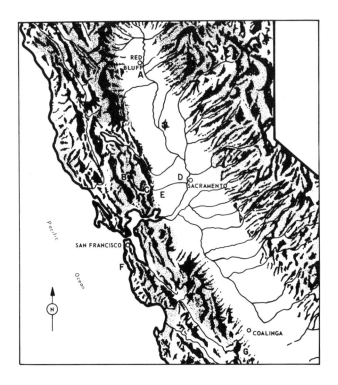

*Figure 2. Collection areas in Northern California, desig-
nated by letters A–F*

Methods of Estimation

To estimate the frequency of outcrossing, α, and the gene frequency, q, a sample of seeds was collected from S- and ss plants and grown separately. The frequency of ss arising in progeny from S- will be designated by the statistic x, and the frequency of Ss arising in progeny from ss will be designated by the statistic y. Expectations are given by

$$E(x) = (q - u)(1 - \alpha + 2\alpha q)/2(1 - u) \qquad (9)$$

and

$$E(y) = \alpha(p) \qquad (10)$$

where u is the estimate of R, the frequency of recessives in the natural population (3). Equating observations x and y to their respective expectations and eliminating α gives q as the appropriate root of the quadratic

$$[1 - 2y]q^2 + [2(uy + xu - x) + y - u - 1]q + \tag{11}$$
$$[2x(1 - u) + u(1 - y)] = 0$$

The solution $\hat{q}$ can be used to obtain the estimate of α, given by

$$\hat{\alpha} = y/(1 - q) \tag{12}$$

This assumes that the outcrossing is random.

The genotypic frequencies D, H, and R are given by

$$\hat{R} = u$$
$$\hat{H} = 2(q - u) \tag{13}$$
$$\hat{D} = 1 + \mu - 2q$$

Expectations for Equation 13 were given by Equation 3. These observations and expectations can be substituted into Equation 8 to obtain estimates of the relative fitness coefficients. However, these estimates are based on the assumption of genotypic frequency equilibrium. Since this

Figure 3.   Collection areas in Southern California, designated by letters G–P

assumption is most unlikely during such colonizing episodes, the estimates must be treated as the crudest of first approximations.

Experimental Results

At present 29 estimates of α, q, and F have been obtained from populations included in Tables I, II, and III. The outcrossing frequencies, α, and inbreeding coefficients, F, are summarized in Figure 4. The distributions suggest that, in spite of theoretical expectations, these populations are far from totally inbred, and the average rate of cross-fertilization

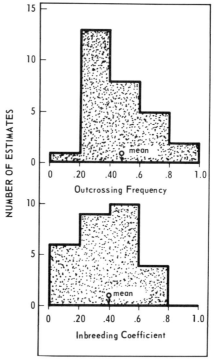

Figure 4. Frequency histograms for combined estimates of α, the rate of cross-fertilization, and F, the coefficient of inbreeding

is approximately 50%. Fitness values were also estimated for these populations and are summarized in Figure 5. The results presented in these figures do not deviate from results obtained from noncolonizing species (3, 11, 12).

The populations under study all occupy habitats with varying degrees of disturbance. Attempts were made to locate populations in habitats with a minimum of disturbance. The populations with the least

Table I. Frequencies and Binomial Standard Errors for Plants with Dominant Seed Coat Band, S-, from Northern California in 1968

Geographic Area	Population	Frequency S−
A	Red Bluff 1	0.47 ± 0.04
	Tehema 1	0.79 ± 0.04
	Corning 1	0.13 ± 0.03
	Orland 1	0.77 ± 0.04
	2	0.77 ± 0.06
B	Upper Putah 1	0.26 ± 0.04
	2	0.10 ± 0.03
	3	0.41 ± 0.04
	4	0.70 ± 0.02
D	El Macero 1	0.05 ± 0.03
	3	0.02 ± 0.02
	Davis 1	0.03 ± 0.02
E	Vacaville 1	0.33 ± 0.02
	2	0.03 ± 0.02
F	San Gregorio 1	0

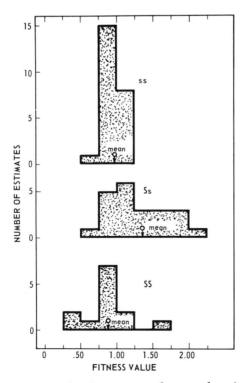

Figure 5. Approximate fitness values for the genotypes SS, Ss, *and* ss

apparent disturbance were the Mace Populations, Vacaville-2, San Gregorio, and Tar Canyon. The remaining populations colonized recently and are ruderals. A classification of populations as to relatively disturbed *vs.* relatively undisturbed is necessarily subjective, and for the undisturbed cases based on limited numbers of observations. The comparison, Figure 6, suggests that the S/s locus is at least as variable in more disturbed roadside habitats as it is in the less disturbed habitats. Furthermore, the few flower color polymorphisms that were found occurred only in disturbed sites.

Summary

The interrelationships among natural selection, inbreeding, and genetic drift are reviewed with emphasis on colonization. Genetic variation at four loci in *Lupinus succulentus* exists in samples taken from California. A mathematical model was developed, and estimators were derived for gene frequency, heterozygote frequency, rate of cross-fertilization, and a coefficient of inbreeding. These parameters were estimated for 29 populations. The results indicate that (1) variation is nearly always present for the S/s locus affecting seed pigmentation, but generally absent for the three loci affecting flower pigmentation; (2) variation is not reduced in populations from recently colonized sites; (3) self-fertilization ranges from nearly 0 to nearly 100%, with mean near 0.50; and, (4) inbreeding coefficients vary from 0 to 0.80, with mean near 0.40.

The results do not suggest that man's disturbance of the environment has had any deleterious effect on the genetic structure of *Lupinus soc-*

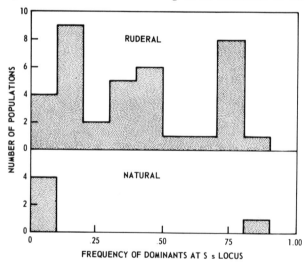

Figure 6. Frequency of S- in populations considered natural and ruderal

Table II.   Frequencies and Binomial Standard Errors for Plants with Dominant Seed Coat Band, S-, from Geographic Area C in Northern California

Population	Year	Frequency S−
Lower Putah 1	1962	0.38 ± 0.07
	1963	0.76 ± 0.05
Lower Putah 2	1962	0.46 ± 0.09
	1963	0.36 ± 0.06
	1966	0.42 ± 0.05
	1967	0.42 ± 0.05
Lower Putah 3	1966	0.14 ± 0.04
	1967	0.18 ± 0.04
Lower Putah 4	1966	0.14 ± 0.03
	1967	0.14 ± 0.03
Lower Putah 5	1966	0.10 ± 0.03
	1967	0.14 ± 0.03
Mace 11	1962	0
30	1967	0.01 ± 0.01

Table III.   Frequencies and Binomial Standard Errors for Plants with Dominant Seed Coat Band, S-, from Southern California in 1968

Geographic Area	Population	Frequency S−
G	Tar Canyon 2	0.81 ± 0.04
	Reef City 1	0.17 ± 0.06
H	San Luis Obispo 1	0.27 ± 0.04
J	Lompac 1	0.85 ± 0.07
	2	0.46 ± 0.04
	Solvang 1	0.71 ± 0.10
K	Santa Barbara 1	0.62 ± 0.06
	2	0.70 ± 0.07
L	Castaic 1	0.36 ± 0.06
	2	0.70 ± 0.04
M	Murrieta 1	0.52 ± 0.10
N	Vista 1	0.32 ± 0.04
P	Misson Bay 1	0

culentus populations. On the contrary, this species has been an opportunistic colonizer of these new habitats. However, *Lupinus succulentus* was chosen for study because it has been a successful colonizer. These conclusions, if general at all, therefore, apply to successful colonizing species and not to those that cannot adapt to environmental disturbances and are now threatened with extinction.

74   AIR POLLUTION DAMAGE TO VEGETATION

Literature Cited

1. Wright, S., "The Interpretation of Population Structure by F-Statistics with Special Regard to Systems of Mating," *Evolution* (1965) **19**, 395.
2. Fyfe, J. L., Bailey, N. T. J., "Plant Breeding Studies in Leguminous Forage Crops. I. Natural Crossing in Winter Beans," *J. Agr. Sci.* (1951) **41**, 371.
3. Harding, J., "Genetics of Lupinus. II. The Selective Disadvantage of the Pink Flower Color Mutant in *Lupinus nanus*," *Evolution* (1970) **24**, 120.
4. "Genes and Mutations," Cold Spring Harbor Symposium on Quantitative Biology, No. 16, 1951.
5. Kempthorne, O., "An Introduction to Genetic Statistics," Wiley, New York, 1957.
6. Tucker, C. L., Harding, J., "Quantitative Studies on Mating Systems. II. Estimation of Fitness Parameters in a Population of *Phaseolus lunatus*," *Heredity* (1965) **20**, 393.
7. Mayr, E., "Animal Species and Evolution," Harvard University Press, Cambridge, Mass., 1963.
8. Baker, H. G., "Self-Compatibility and Establishment after 'Long-Distance' Dispersal," *Evolution* (1955) **9**, 347.
9. Stebbins, G. L., "Self-Fertilization and Population Variability in the Higher Plants," *Amer. Nat.* (1957) **91**, 337.
10. Stebbins, G. L., "Colonizing Species of the Native California Flora," in "The Genetics of Colonizing Species," Academic Press, New York, 1965.
11. Weil, J., Allard, R. W., "The Mating System and Genetic Variability in Natural Populations of *Collinsia heterophylla*," *Evolution* (1965) **18**, 515.
12. Vasek, F. C., "Outcrossing in Natural Populations. III. The Deer Creek Population of *Clarkia exilis*," *Evolution* (1967) **21**, 241.

RECEIVED September 23, 1971.

Selecting and Breeding Plants for Increased Resistance to Air Pollutants

EDWARD J. RYDER

Agricultural Research Service, Western Region, U. S. Department of
Agriculture, Salinas, Calif. 93901

*Few plant species have been investigated for variation in
reaction to air pollution. Evidence for a genetic basis for
resistance has been found in several species. Little is known
of plant response to two or more pollutants and of the
physical basis for resistance. Breeding new varieties resistant
to air pollutants may be carried on despite the absence of
some fundamental knowledge. Breeding procedures include
selection of resistant plants out of an existing population
and crossing of sensitive with resistant plants followed by
selection of new types combining favorable characteristics
of both parents. Present breeding programs are listed.
Future needs and prospects are discussed.*

Air pollutants cause plant damage which varies both in type and
degree. A few crop, ornamental, and forest species have shown a
variability in the degree of damage so that some varieties within these
species may be classed as resistant and others as susceptible. This variability probably exists in many species in which it has not yet been
demonstrated. Further, in a few species this variability is at least in part
genetically based. Therefore, the opportunity exists to select those plants
resistant to the toxicants and to breed new varieties which can be successfully grown in a polluted atmosphere. Obviously, this solves only
part of the air pollution problem. Resistant varieties will alleviate some
effect of air pollution on plants but will not eliminate the pollutants
themselves.

However, this paper is designed to discuss the use of plant breeding
techniques to modify the heredity of a plant species, enabling it to produce a crop or to survive in a hostile atmosphere. Hostile atmospheres,
in the literal sense, are not new to the plant world. Man himself first

became conscious of them when he saw his crops dying for reasons unknown to him. Later, he discovered that the air carried insects and disease organisms and that it was these which were destroying his crops. So he began to develop methods of breeding resistance to these pests. Now he finds he must cope with a new kind of hostility in the air, in addition to those with which he has become reasonably familiar. Fortunately, it appears that breeding for air pollution resistance may be accomplished with essentially the same techniques as for the more traditional pests.

Two questions may be asked at the outset. Which plant species are damaged by air pollution? Are there sources of genetic variation available in these species?

Few plant species upon which man depends for his food, clothing, shelter, and aesthetic pleasure have been investigated. Researchers have dealt principally with the identification of air pollutants, the effects they have on plants, and some of the conditions under which these effects may vary. One of these conditions, to use the term broadly, is the genetic state of a species with respect to its reaction to air pollution. We know that some species show resistance, but there is a considerably greater number about which we know little or nothing.

Resistant Plant Species

One must distinguish between resistant species and resistance within species. The use of the former as substitutes for susceptible species in parks, industrial areas, and other urban settings is more properly discussed in ecological engineering terms. We are primarily interested here in the identification and use of resistant variants within species and the use of several plant breeding techniques to obtain new and improved resistant varieties. These techniques include selection of resistant plants within varieties, selection of resistant varieties within species, and crosses between varieties with subsequent selection of improved progenies.

In this context, then, variation in resistance to some pollutants has been described in several species (Table I). The list does not include species having resistance to the various pesticides but only species resistant to those pollutants usually associated with automobile combustion and industrial processes.

Another clarification regarding the designation of species as resistant or sensitive should be made. It can be reasonably assumed that many more species than those in which resistance has been noted will in fact include varieties which are resistant. Most studies which have been made on the effects of air pollutants on plants have been based on a relatively few plants of a relatively few varieties.

Evaluating the entire species as resistant or sensitive on this basis is apt to be misleading for the obvious reason of sampling error. In fact, in those studies in which several varieties have been tested, it has usually been found that variety differences exist. Therefore it may be assumed

Table I. Crop, Ornamental, and Forest Species in Which Variation in Sensitivity to the Pollutants Named Has Been Observed

Species	Pollutant	Reference
Crop Species		
Alfalfa (*Medicago sativa* L.)	Ozone	*19*
Citrus (*Citrus* sp)	Fluoride	*20*
Cucumber (*Cucumis sativus* L.)	Ozone	*21*
Grain sorghum (*Sorghum vulgare* Pers.)	Fluoride	*22*
Green bean (*Phaseolus vulgaris* L.)	Ozone, ambient air	*23*
Lettuce (*Lactuca sativa* L.)	Ozone	*18*
Oats (*Avena sativa* L.)	Ozone	*24*
Onion (*Allium cepa* L.)	Ozone	*3*
Potato (*Solanum tuberosum* L.)	Ozone	*24*
Radish (*Raphanus sativus* L.)	Ozone	*25*
Red clover (*Trifolium pratense* L.)	Ozone	*26*
Spinach (*Spinacia oleracea* L.)	Oxidant	*14*
Sweet corn (*Zea mays* L.)	Oxidant	*27*
Tobacco (*Nicotiana tabacum* L.)	Ozone	*28*
Tomato (*Lycopersicon esculentum* Mill.)	Ozone	*25*
Turfgrass (Several species)	Ozone, SO_2	*29*
White bean (*Phaseolus vulgaris* L.)	Oxidant	*6*
Ornamental Species		
Coleus (*Coleus* sp.)	Ozone	*21*
Gladiolus (*Gladiolus* sp.)	Fluoride	*30*
Petunia (*Petunia hybrida* Vilm.)	Ozone, PAN, SO_2, NO_2, irrad exhaust	*7*
Forest Species		
Douglas fir (*Pseudotsuga taxifolia* Brit.)	SO_2	*31*
Eastern white pine (*Pinus strobus* L.)	Ozone, SO_2	*32*
Larch (*Larix* sp.)	SO_2	*33*
Lodgepole pine (*Pinus contorta* Dougl.)	SO_2	*31*
Norway spruce (*Picea abies* L.)	SO_2, fluoride	*34*
Ponderosa pine (*Pinus ponderosa* Laws)	Oxidant, fluoride	*35*
Scotch pine (*Pinus sylvestris* L.)	SO_2, fluoride	*34*

that variety screening among species named in various lists, for example, by Jacobson and Hill (*1*), will disclose that variety differences do exist and that few species can be properly classified after testing one or two varieties. Hill, Heggestad, and Linzon (*2*) do note that their list of species sensitive to ozone is based on "certain varieties or clones."

In only one species has a gene for resistance been identified: a single dominant gene confers resistance to ozone-induced tipburn in the onion (3). Information about the other species listed in Table I is less specific. Fairly substantial evidence for a genetic basis for resistance to ozone weather fleck in tobacco has been found although specific genes have not been identified (4, 5). On the other hand, oxidant bronzing of white beans has been observed, but is described in the following way: "... within a relatively uniform crop, damage is often not uniform" (6). This is suggestive but not critical evidence for genetic resistance. Similar evaluations in other crops indicate that although the presumption of a genetic basis for resistance to air pollution damage is a reasonable one, hard evidence is lacking. In most species in which air pollution injury has been observed, there is no reported evidence for resistance.

Certain other types of evidence of plant response are also scarce. We know little about the response by the various crop species to mixtures of air pollutants or to two or more pollutants acting on the plants at different times. Feder et al. (7) report differences in sensitivity of petunia varieties to ozone, sulfur dioxide, PAN, nitrogen dioxide, and irradiated auto exhaust. There seemed, in addition, to be a correlated response to the different gases such that a variety relatively sensitive to one was relatively sensitive to one or more of the others.

Zimmerman and Hitchcock (8) exposed several plant species to SO_2 and fluoride. They found that some species were equally sensitive to both, some equally resistant to both, and some resistant to one and sensitive to the other. There is little other evidence of this type. An important question therefore is: in an area in which a crop may be exposed to several toxicants, how many genes will be necessary to protect the crop against all of them?

Little is known of the physical basis for resistance. In onions resistant to tipburn, the stomates close when exposed to ozone, thus preventing the entrance of the gas into the tissues. They reopen when the air is free of pollutant. The stomates of sensitive plants remain open, permitting the gas to enter and injure the parenchyma cells, leading to burning and collapse of tissue (3). In another study, with pinto beans, Dugger et al. (9), intimate that resistance to ozone might be related to high soluble sugar content in the leaves.

Fortunately, programs for developing resistant varieties may be carried on despite a lack of genetic and physiological knowledge. There may be some loss of efficiency and some uncertainty as to direction, but progress in selecting improved types may be made.

For example, if genetic variation exists in a crop plant population, it will become apparent under the environmental stress of a siege of pollution. Some individuals will survive the attack with no or minimum injury, and it is usually a simple matter to select these. Progeny from the selected individuals may then be grown and subjected to the pollutant again. If progeny from sensitive parents are also selected and subjected to the pollutant, and if the sensitive progeny are sensitive and the resistant progeny are resistant, this is evidence of a real genetic difference. The next step is to increase the resistant plants at the expense of the sensitive ones and replace the original variable population with a new population all of whose members are resistant. This successfully completes the program.

Often, however, it is necessary to resort to a more complex procedure. If none of the plants in the population of interest is resistant, the breeder must look outside that population for a source of resistance, either in another variety or in a wild relative. The resistant plants in the second population may be susceptible to a disease, may yield less than desired, have poor color or quality, or be sensitive to heat or cold.

Then the plant breeder must make a cross between the variety with desirable production characteristics and the variety or line carrying the resistance. In subsequent generations, he must select toward a new variety combining the desirable characteristics of the two parents. This program may take 10 years or longer. During its progress, he must subject his progeny to a screening test designed to select plants which are resistant to air pollution and reject the others. This might be done in a chamber into which he would meter an appropriate gas to expose the plants he wishes to test. He must also select each year for the various agronomic traits which have commercial value. These might include characters like high yield, attractive appearance, resistance to diseases or insects or various kinds of physiological breakdown, favorable processing characteristics, favorable fruit or seed characteristics, and so on. Each year, progeny must be planted in the field, notes taken on the various characters, selections made on the basis of these notes, and seed harvested from selected plants to be planted the following year. If the ambient atmosphere is a dependable source of pollutant, resistant plants can also be selected in the field. Complicating the process is the environment, which may enhance or negate a specific trait. The breeder may discover the following season that he has selected plants which are not as desirable genetically as they appeared. He may also be reasonably certain that he rejected some which were better than they appeared. Finally, after several years of selection, a breeding line may be developed which is resistant to the air pollutant and appears to have all the desired commercial characteristics.

The breeder then contemplates releasing the line as a new commercial variety. It must be remembered that when a cross is made in which the resistant parent is a breeding line, a commercial variety from another area, a variety from another country, or a wild relative from anywhere, the breeder runs the risk of introducing deleterious genes into the breeding population. If he is lucky, the effects of these genes will be noted somewhere along the breeding process, and the plant carriers can be eliminated. Sometimes, however, the undesirable genes do not show themselves until after the variety is officially released. For example, the new variety may be highly susceptible to a disease which had not infected the older varieties or had not been a problem during the breeding program, or the breeding program may have been conducted during a period of relatively warm, dry years, and the selections may be adapted to those climatic conditions. If the weather becomes relatively cool and damp after the variety is released, it may no longer be well adapted.

A possibly unique problem in air pollution breeding research is that in selecting for resistance to visible symptoms, a breeder may select toward increased ability of the plant to absorb the pollutant without showing injury. In a food plant, if this level is toxic to man or animals, he has negated his original breeding purpose. This may occur in breeding for resistance to fluoride, which does accumulate in plant tissues (10).

On the other hand, a possibly unique benefit in air pollution breeding research may derive from selection over the years for increased yield or fitness in an area where air pollution has long been a problem. The breeder may have unknowingly selected partly for resistance to chronic injury or growth retardation (11). This might occur in species where reproduction occurs in the same area as production of the crop for commercial use, as well as in natural stands. It would not occur where the crop is grown in a polluted area and reproduced in another, nonpolluted area where no selective force would act. Where this type of selection did occur, a new breeding program specifically oriented toward air pollution resistance would therefore benefit.

New Breeding Programs

The resistance to ozone-induced tipburn in onions mentioned earlier is being incorporated into commercial onion varieties primarily for the Midwest at the University of Wisconsin (12). In a program at the University of Tennessee, dark green vigorous trees have been selected in stands of eastern white pine in which most trees have died because of sensitivity to ozone, SO_2, and automobile exhaust constituents. Crosses have been made to determine the genetics of resistance, and a formal breeding orchard of resistant trees has been established (13).

Resistance to SO_2 and ozone in spinach, potatoes, and tomatoes appears to be genetic, and programs for incorporating resistance into new varieties are under way at the USDA Plant Industry Station in Beltsville, Md. (*14*).

At Pennsylvania State University, breeding for resistance to ozone and SO_2 in scotch pine is underway. Resistance seems to be genetic. Selections for resistance were made initially in a fumigation nursery and will be tested further in stands planted near pollutant sources. Crosses are being made for genetic studies as well as for selection for resistance and for favorable ornamental traits of crown form, branching habit, and needle color (*15*).

Photochemical injury to ponderosa pine in the San Bernardino National Forest of California is a serious problem there. Screening for resistance to ozone is being carried on in preparation for conducting a formal breeding program (*16*).

Two programs for increased resistance to weather fleck in tobacco are in progress—one in Canada and one in the Connecticut Valley. The Canadian program involves the development of resistant flue-cured tobacco varieties (*5*), and the U. S. program under G. S. Taylor of the Connecticut Agriculture Experiment Station is for cigar wrapper varieties.

These examples comprise most of the projects in air pollution breeding research in North America (known as of January 1972). Obviously, considerably more work needs to be done.

Future Prospects

No one knows how many crop varieties are affected adversely by air pollution beyond the few which have been studied. Thus, it is important that surveys continue to be made of the susceptibility of useful plant species, particularly those grown in areas of high air pollution incidence and in areas of potentially high incidence. These surveys should include all the major air toxicants known to cause injury to plants in each area. The genetic state of each crop must be assessed, and, in those crops which are uniformly susceptible, it will be necessary to screen noncommercial materials for resistance, possibly including wild relatives. Appropriate breeding programs can then be started.

Two important facets of this proposed program should be expanded. First, it is relatively easy to screen for visible injury or damage to plant tissues. In most cases, seedlings or small plants may be evaluated, and large numbers of plants can be handled in fumigant chambers. Increasing evidence, however, shows that chronic injury in the form of reduced yields may result from exposure to pollutant gases at chronic low doses. Other injuries such as weakened plant structures and increased disease susceptibility may also result. It is considerably more difficult to evaluate these responses. They usually must be measured and analyzed statistically, requiring large numbers of plants in replicated field and greenhouse trials. The plants often need to be grown to maturity. The requirements of time and expense and the uncertainty of the accuracy of the evaluation will be greatly increased over those of an acute injury screening program. So too will the length of time and expense of the breeding program. This is not a unique problem for plant breeders. Most programs involving characters which need to be measured rather than classified have these difficulties.

Secondly, if we assume that air pollution problems will get worse before they get better, we can also assume that some areas not now faced with a pollution problem will soon have one. For example, one of the major vegetable growing areas in the United States, the Salinas Valley, Calif., may face this prospect. The Salinas Valley now is the last clean major air shed in the state of California (17). How long this will be true is not known. All the prerequisites for an eventual air pollution problem are there: a climatic and geographic configuration which produces temperature inversions during the growing season, a potential for industrial and population growth, and nearly 200,000 acres of crops, most of which are sensitive to air pollution damage. These include lettuce, celery, tomato, radish, bean, spinach, potato, wine grape, onion, carrot, and sugarbeet.

The potential vulnerability of lettuce is of particular concern. Over 50,000 acres of head lettuce are grown each year in the Salinas Valley. This represents nearly one-third of the nation's lettuce crop. Lettuce is one of the major vegetable crops grown in this country; only potatoes and tomatoes exceed it in acreage, production, and dollar value. As a species, it is considered sensitive to PAN, SO_2, and nitrogen oxides (1). However, Reinert et al. (18) have shown differential sensitivity to ozone among eight varieties, which indicates the potentiality of breeding for resistance. There is great need to identify varieties resistant to PAN, nitrogen oxides, and ozone on a greater scale than has already been done and to breed new resistant varieties if the important commercial varieties are not resistant. An opportunity rare in plant breeding history exists to fill a need before it becomes critical.

The genetic and breeding proposals described here are probably of a scope which is equivalent to the present totality of plant breeding programs in the United States. Again the basic responsibility for alleviating the effects of air pollutants on plants lies elsewhere: at the sources. This responsibility must be fulfilled. Plant breeders already have plenty to do. There are many other problems which urgently need solving. It would be desirable to be able to work at these problems in an atmosphere benevolent to both plants and plant breeders.

Literature Cited

1. Jacobson, J. S., Hill, A. C., Eds., "Recognition of Air Pollution Injury to Vegetation: A Pictorial Atlas," Informative Report No. 1, Air Pollution Control Association, 1970.
2. Hill, A. C., Heggestad, H. E., Linzon, S. N., "Ozone," in "Recognition of Air Pollution Injury to Vegetation: a Pictorial Atlas," pp. B1–22, Informative Report No. 1, Air Pollution Control Association, 1970.
3. Engle, R. L., Gabelman, W. H., "Inheritance and Mechanism of Resistance to Ozone Damage in Onion, *Allium cepa* L.," *Proc. Amer. Soc. Hort. Sci.* (1966) **89,** 423.
4. Sand, S. A., "Weather Fleck in Shade Tobacco as a Problem of Interactions Between Genes and the Environment," *Tobacco Sci.* (1960) **4,** 137.
5. Povilaitis, B., "Gene Effects for Tolerance to Weather Fleck in Tobacco," *Can. J. Genet. Cytol.* (1967) **9,** 327.
6. Haas, J. H., "Relation of Crop Maturity and Physiology to Air Pollution Incited Bronzing of *Phaseolus vulgaris*," *Phytopathology* (1970) **60,** 407.
7. Feder, W. A., Fox, F. L., Heck, W. W., Campbell, F. J., "Varietal Responses of Petunia to Several Air Pollutants," *Plant Dis. Rept.* (1969) **53,** 506.
8. Zimmerman, P. W., Hitchcock, A. E., "Susceptibility of Plants to Hydrofluoric Acid and Sulfur Dioxide Gases," *Contrib. Boyce Thompson Inst.* (1956) **18,** 263.
9. Dugger, W. M., Jr., Taylor, O. C., Cardiff, E., Thompson, C. R., "Relationships Between Carbohydrate Content and Susceptibility of Pinto Bean Plants to Ozone Damage," *Proc. Amer. Soc. Hort. Sci.* (1962) **81,** 304.
10. MacLean, D. C., Schneider, R. E., Weinstein, L. H., "Accumulation of Fluoride by Forage Crops," *Contrib. Boyce Thompson Inst.* (1969) **24,** 165.
11. Heggestad, H. E., Heck, W. W., "Nature, Extent and Variation of Plant Response to Air Pollutants," in press.
12. Gabelman, W. H., personal communication, 1970.
13. Thor, E., personal communication, 1970.
14. Webb, R. E., personal communication, 1970.
15. Gerhold, H. D., Palpant, E. H., "Prospects for Breeding Ornamental Scotch Pines Resistant to Air Pollutants," *Proc. 6th Central States Tree Imp. Conf.* (1968) 34.
16. Miller, P. R., personal communication, 1970.
17. Middleton, J. T., "Trends in Air Pollution Damage," *Arch. Environ. Health* (1964) **8,** 19.
18. Reinert, R. A., Tingey, D. T., Carter, H. B., "Sensitivity of Lettuce Varieties to Ozone," *HortScience* (1970) **5,** 334.
19. Howell, R. K., Devine, T. E., Hanson, C. H., "Resistance of Selected Alfalfa Strains to Ozone," *Crop Sci.* (1971) **11,** 114.
20. Brewer, R. F., Creveling, R. R., Guillemet, F. B., Sutherland, F. H., "The Effects of Hydrogen Fluoride Gas on Seven Citrus Varieties," *Proc. Amer. Soc. Hort. Sci.* (1960) **75,** 236.
21. Feder, W. A., personal communication, 1971.
22. Schneider, R. E., MacLean, D. C., "Relative Susceptibility of Seven Grain Sorghum Hybrids to Hydrogen Fluoride," *Contrib. Boyce Thompson Inst.* (1970) **24,** 241.
23. Howell, R. K., "Differential Responses of Bean Cultivars to Ozone and Ambient Air," *HortScience* (1970) **5,** 334.
24. Brennan, E., Leone, I. A., Daines, R. H., "The Importance of Variety in Ozone Plant Damage," *Plant Dis. Rept.* (1964) **48,** 923.
25. Reinert, R. A., Tingey, D. T., Carter, H. B., "Varietal Sensitivity of Tomato and Radish to Ozone," *HortScience* (1969) **4,** 189.

26. Brennan, E., Leone, I. A., Halisky, P. M., "Response of Forage Legumes to Ozone Fumigations," *Phytopathology* (1969) **59**, 1458.
27. Cameron, J. W., Johnson, H., Jr., Taylor, O. C., Otto, H. W., "Differential Susceptibility of Sweet Corn Hybrids to Field Injury by Air Pollution," *HortScience* (1970) **5**, 217.
28. Heggestad, H. E., Burleson, F. R., Middleton, J. T., Darley, E. F., "Leaf Injury on Tobacco Varieties Resulting from Ozone, Ozonated Hexene-1 and Ambient Air of Metropolitan Areas," *Int. J. Air Wat. Pollut.* (1964) **8**, 1.
29. Halisky, P. M., Brennan, E., "Response of Turfgrass Cultivars to Ozone and Sulfur Dioxide in the Atmosphere," *Phytopathology* (1970) **60**, 1544.
30. Thomas, M. D., "Gas Damage to Plants," *Annu. Rev. Plant Physiol.* (1951) **2**, 293.
31. Enderlein, H., Vogl, M., "Experimentelle Untersuchungen uber die SO_2-Empfindlichkeit der Nadeln verschiedener Koniferen," *Arch. Forst.* (1966) **15**, 1207.
32. Berry, C. R., Hepting, G. H., "Injury to Eastern White Pine by Unidentified Atmospheric Constituents," *Forest Sci.* (1964) **10**, 2.
33. Schonbach, H., Dassler, H. G., Enderlein, H., Bellmann, E., Kastner, W., "Uber den unterschiedlichen Einfluss von Schwefeldioxyd auf die Nadeln verschiedener 2-jahriger Larchenkreuzungen," *Zuchter* (1964) **34**, 312.
34. Rohmeder, E., Merz, W., von Schonborn, A., "Zuchtung von gegen Industrieabgase relativ resistenten Fichten and Kiefernsorten," *Forstw. Cbl.* (1962) **81**, 321.
35. Hepting, G. H., "Damage to Forests from Air Pollution," *J. Forest.* (1964) **62**, 630.

RECEIVED September 23, 1971.

8

Chemistry and Community Composition

MICHAEL G. BARBOUR

Botany Department, University of California, Davis, Calif. 95616

The results of recent ecological research seem to have given new insight and credibility to Frederick Clements' 50-year-old postulate that community members are so interdependent and vital to each other that they form a living whole, a superorganism. This research indicates that those plant and animal species which comprise a given community are associated—and others excluded—by factors other than the chance arrival of reproductive propagules or the strictly physical factors of the environment. The organisms are, additionally, collectively sieved through a network of chemical interactions. However, all the evidence for chemical regulation of community composition cannot be accepted at face value. From selected references, sample evidence indicative of chemical control at the producer, consumer, and decomposer levels is presented. Considerable ecological, rather than chemical, work is now needed to indicate the real significance to community composition and dynamics of many chemical interactions reported.

Other chapters in this book deal with the effects of man-made chemicals on individual plants, populations, and communities—man-made chemicals in the sense that they are byproducts of technology. To understand how such chemicals may have a subtle or dramatic effect on a community, this paper reviews the effect of naturally occurring chemical effluents—those produced by the community itself.

Most ecologists define a community as a group of plant and animal organisms which occur together in a given habitat. Within a relatively large geographic area, this same assemblage of species repeats itself wherever the same habitat recurs. Regardless of the complexity of a community, there are usually three basic components: producers, consumers, and decomposers. Producers are green plants and photosynthetic bacteria at the base of the food chain. Consumers are parasites, herbivores, and predators. Decomposers include some bacteria, fungi, and animals which utilize dead organic matter for energy.

Most definitions of a community add that the associated organisms are somehow interdependent and are not associated by chance (1). The concept of interdependence was taken to its extreme by the American ecologist Frederick Clements, who equated certain communities with organisms. Like an organism, he wrote in 1916 (2), such a community ". . . arises, grows, matures, and dies. Furthermore, each . . . is able to reproduce itself, repeating with essential fidelity the stages of its development . . . comparable in its chief features with the life-history of an individual plant." Many biologists disagree with this view, but my purpose here is not to define a community; it is to investigate what holds it together, what molds its composition.

Recent research has shown that chemicals may provide an important medium for interactions and interdependence of community members. It is ironic that this evidence should support, in some ways, Clements' view of the community, for he thought of interaction as being only of a physical nature. However, in some cases it seems that new information has been accumulated too rapidly to allow digestion; sweeping statements about the significance of chemical interactions to community composition and dynamics have been made without real cause-and-effect data. This paper summarizes sample evidence for chemical control and analyzes whether it has ecological significance. This review is done at all three community levels—producer, consumer, and decomposer. At the consumer level, herbivore–predator interactions are not examined. This is not a thorough literature review; attempts at such a review already exist (3).

The Producer–Decomposer Level

To a large degree, decomposers in the soil and litter beneath a community are affected by the species of plants shedding the litter and penetrating the soil with roots. As Eyre (4) has pointed out, soils beneath northern conifer forests are acidic because conifer litter is acidic and its decomposition influences soil pH. Fungi, as a result, dominate the soil microflora while bacteria dominate more neutral soil beneath deciduous forests. There are also differences even within one conifer forest: pine needles are much more acidic than spruce, and the soil beneath most pine species has less decomposer activity and is almost devoid of earthworms, in comparison with soil beneath spruce species.

The presence of certain fungi in the soil is of critical importance to many higher plants, because the fungi play a symbiotic role with their roots. Root tips of trees, shrubs, and herbs become infected with soil fungi. The resulting swollen tips are called mycorrhizae. The relationship is not parasitic, but an exchange of material does result: the fungus gains carbohydrates, and the root gains mineral nutrients. Absorption of water and nutrients is dramatically increased by the presence of the fungus (5). In a recent review, Scott (6) estimated that up to 80% of all flowering plants have mycorrhizae. Apparently, the same fungal mass can infect more than one plant, and the result is rapid translocation of materials in the soil. Woods and Brock (7) injected ^{45}Ca and ^{32}P into a freshly cut stump of red maple and collected leaves from nearby trees in the forest during the following week. They found that both isotopes were transferred in the soil to 19 other taxonomically diverse trees and shrubs. The rate of transfer was too rapid to be caused by simple diffusion alone. They concluded that mycorrhizal fungi may have been responsible, and that ". . . it would seem logical to regard the root mass of a forest . . . as a single functional unit. Inability of a species to enter into a 'mutual benefit society,' one in which minerals and other mobile materials are exchanged between roots, could have a negative survival value."

Apart from pH, higher plants affect soil chemistry by passively contributing a variety of inorganic and organic compounds to the soil. Apparently, plants are very leaky systems. Carlisle *et al.* (8) analyzed the nutrient content in rain water falling directly to the ground and in rain water falling through the leaf canopy of sessile oak (*Quercus petraea*). Apart from nitrogen, throughfall contained a higher concentration of nutrients: phosphorus, for example, was more than doubled, potassium was increased nearly ninefold, sodium was increased by half. The nutrients had been passively leached from the leaves by rain water; they would ordinarily be carried down to the soil and accumulate there. Tukey (9) has shown that larger molecules can also be leached from leaves. He grew seedlings and cuttings of 150 species in nutrient culture with certain radioisotopes in it, then leached the plants by atomized mist or immersion in pure water for up to 24 hr. The leachate was channeled through an anion–cation exchange resin and analyzed. It contained 14 elements, including such essential nutrients as iron, calcium, phosphorus, potassium, nitrogen, and magnesium; seven sugars; some pectic substances; 23 amino acids; and 15 organic acids, including virtually all the acids in the Krebs cycle of respiration.

Leaves of many species also give off volatile oils which can be directly adsorbed by soil or be carried down in rain. von Rudloff (10), for example, reported that the quality and quantity of oils in needles of white spruce (*Picea gauca*) were relatively constant over a large range of territory. We will return to some of those 18 compounds or groups later:

α-pinene, myrcene, 1,8-cineole, and camphor. Went (11) has commented on blue hazes associated with conifer forests and some other vegetation types. He suggested that they are caused by a reaction between ozone and volatile terpenes (e.g., pinene), and that they might have a great effect on the heat balance of the earth, let alone on soil chemistry.

In a number of papers, Rice has dealt with the effect of specific plant products on the activity of soil bacteria. Abandoned crop land in Oklahoma reverts to prairie through a sequence of successional communities that may require 30 or more years (12). The first stage, lasting 2–3 years, is composed of pioneer weeds such as amaranth (*Amaranthus retroflexus*), sunflower (*Helianthus annuus*), ragweed (*Ambrosia psilostachya*), and crabgrass (*Digitaria sanguinalis*). Some of these species are natives, others are introductions. This community is then displaced by one dominated by native annual grasses, such as *Aristida oligantha*, which maintains itself for as long as 15 years, then is itself displaced by third and fourth communities. Rice and his co-workers wondered if the course of succession could be directed by chemical interactions in particular interactions affecting nitrogen-fixing and nitrifying bacteria.

Rice (13) made aqueous extracts of flowers, leaves, roots, and stems of 14 pioneer weed species, and tested them for inhibitory effect on strains of *Azotobacter, Nitrobacter,* and *Rhizobium.* All proved inhibitory to one or more of the bacterial strains. In 1965, Rice (14) identified the inhibitors in three of the weed species as chlorogenic acid and gallotannin, both polyphenols. Chlorogenic acid is a strong inhibitor of several enzyme systems (phosphorylase, paroxidase, oxidase), and gallotannins are excellent protein precipitants. In a later paper (15), soils beneath two weed species were found to contain large quantities of gallic and tannic acids (over 600 ppm tannic acid). The authors reported that, in laboratory tests, less than 300 ppm tannic acid was effective in reducing symbiotic nitrogen fixation.

Rice claimed that the weed species had less of a demand for nitrogen than later successional species and that the weed stage prolonged itself by inhibiting certain bacteria, thus reducing nitrogen availability in the soil. However, the story is not ecologically complete. Chlorogenic acid and gallotannis are widespread in the plant kingdom (16) and might be expected in prairie grasses as well as in pioneer weeds. Indeed, his data show that extracts of the prairie perennial grass *Andropogon scaparius* were just as toxic to the bacteria as many weed extracts. Further, if the inhibitors are stable in soil (and Rice presented some data to indicate this is so), then why is the weed stage not prolonged beyond 2–3 years?

The reverse of plants' inhibiting bacteria can also occur: byproducts of bacterial metabolism can inhibit higher plants. Phenolics are common products of decomposers; Wang et al. (17) were able to extract and

Table I.   Effect of Overstory Plants on Germination and Establishment
of Jack Pine (*Pinus banksiana*)[a]

Seeds Planted under:	Labora- tory Effect	Germi- nation after One Summer	Survival after Two Summers
Cherry (*Prunus pumila*)		14	6
Wintergreen (*Gaultheria procumbens*)	—	25	17
Goldenrod (*Solidago juncea*)		30	14
Average, inhibitory plants		23	12
Lichens (*Cladonia rangiferina*)		50	18
Calliergonella schreberi		88	25
Trailing arbutus (*Epigaea repens*)	0	91	51
Blueberry (*Vaccinium angustifolium*)		105	11
Bracken (*Pteridium aquilinum*)		144	67
Average, plants of no effect		96	34
Dogwood (*Cornus canadensis*)		143	12
Red pine (*Pinus resinosa*)	+	222	20
Average, stimulatory plants		183	16

[a] 400 seeds were planted beneath each species; in the laboratory, these species
proved inhibitory (−), stimulatory (+), or of no effect on jack pine germination.
Data from Brown (24).

identify a number of phenolics from soils of sugar can fields in Taiwan.
When added in amounts of 0–100 ppm to culture media of seedlings of
sugar cane, corn, wheat, and soybeans, shoot and root growth of most
were impaired at a concentration above 50 ppm. However, from their
data it appeared that natural soil water would not contain more than
12 ppm of such phenolics, so the ecological significance of the laboratory
interaction is doubtful. Patrick and Koch (18) reported that decomposition residues from timothy, corn, rye, and tobacco affected respiration, germination, and growth of tobacco seedlings. They did not, however, identify the toxins or estimate their abundance in soil. In a review,
Brian (19) listed 38 antibiotics which affect germination and plant growth
in low concentration (1–10 ppm); many of these are thought to be formed
and released in the normal soil system. Although of relatively high
molecular weight, they can be taken up by roots and translocated through
a higher plant. Among his list are a number of metabolic inhibitors of
great specificity and potency.

Plant compounds and products of decay also may affect saprophytic
and parasitic fungi. Rennerfelt and Nacht (20) noted that heartwoods
of pines have a fairly high fungicidal resistance, while those of some
other conifers do not. They were able to extract, isolate, and identify
eight heartwood compounds (from four species) which had fungicidal

properties. All were terpenoids and flavinoids. The authors tested six of the compounds on 12 species of major decay fungi and reported major differences in susceptibility. Growth of all fungal species, for example, was reduced to zero by 10 ppm γ-thujaplicin (from *Thuja plicata*) while reaction to pinosylvin (from *Pinus*) was mixed: *Merulius lacrymans* growth was reduced to zero by less than 15 ppm, but growth of *Phiostoma pini* was hardly affected even by 200 ppm. Generally, almost all the fungi were inhibited or killed by normal heartwood concentrations of the compounds. However, the ecological significance of the interaction is not clear. Heartwood of larch, cedar, and *Sequoia* are resistant to decay, but fungicidal compounds have not been extracted from them. Of the four species which the authors did show contained fungicides, they did not comment on whether or not the laboratory-susceptible fungi occur in nature on those species; that is, is there a negative association in nature, as predicted by the laboratory experiments? If the fungicides are effective, why are they of such limited distribution? Are heartwood decomposers species-specific?

The Producer–Producer Level

A number of workers have reported evidence for chemical control of plant distribution, spatial associations between species, and the course of community succession.

One of the most complete studies is that by Muller (*21*) on the spatial relationship between coastal sage (*Salvia leucophylla*) and annual grassland in the Santa Ynez valley of southern California. A number of chaparral species, including sage, dominate the foothills, while annual grasses and herbs dominate the valley floors. However, patches of sage shrubs may occur in the grassland. Beneath those shrubs, and for 1–2 meters beyond the shrub canopy limits, the ground is devoid of herbs and grasses. Even 6–10 meters from the canopy, annuals are stunted. Stunting is not caused by competition for water since shrub roots do not penetrate that far into the grassland, and stunting is observed even in the wettest parts of the year. Nor do soil factors seem responsible for the negative association: major chemical and physical soil factors do not change across the bare zone. Muller was able to show that *Salvia* shrubs emit a number of volatile oils from their leaves and that some of these (principally cineole and camphor) are toxic to germination and growth of surrounding annuals. He was able to detect these substances in the field and to demonstrate that they are adsorbed by the soil and can be retained there for months and that they are able to enter seeds and seedlings through their waxy cuticles. He was not, however, able to detect the same amounts of oils in natural soils that were necessary to produce inhibition in the laboratory.

Muller was also unable to eliminate completely other factors as contributing to maintenance of the bare zones. Bartholomew (22) examined in more detail the influence of mammalian and bird herbivores which reside in the shrub clumps but forage in the grassland. Foraging activity, he reasoned, would increase closer to the shrubs and might be the main cause for maintenance of the bare zone. From seed predation and exclosure experiments, Bartholomew was able to substantiate that hypothesis. Muller (23) agrees that herbivory has some influence on the bare zone but argues that it cannot explain the stunted zone. He adds that ". . . biochemical products are widely, if not universally, involved in biotic interactions . . .," but that the chemical products do not act alone in a vacuum: their activity is modified by other environmental factors such as drought, shading, and grazing.

A short study by Brown (24) implicates the role of species-specific biochemical interactions in the association of forest species. He made aqueous extracts of leaves, fruit, and flowers of 56 species of a pine forest in Michigan dominated by jack pine (*Pinus banksiana*), and he tested their effect on germination of jack pine. Most had no statistically significant effect, but extracts from nine species inhibited germination, and extracts from five others stimulated germination. Using the laboratory results as a predictive model, he planted 400 jack pine seeds under each of 10 species in the field (Table I). In the laboratory, extracts of three of those species inhibited germination, extracts of five had no effect, and extracts of two had a stimulatory effect. In nature, these substances would be leached by rain and deposited in the soil beneath the canopy. The effect of these species on germination in nature did parallel laboratory results: average germination was eight times as great under stimulatory species than under inhibitory species. However, survival, after two summers, did not show that relationship: survival was about equal beneath stimulatory and inhibitory species, and was greatest beneath species of supposedly no effect. Brown indicated that grazing intensity by small mammals probably had more importance to survival of jack pine than did soil chemistry.

Webb *et al.* (25) reported on the successes and failures of plantations of rainforest trees in Australia. Some species, such as those of the conifer *Araucaria*, grow in clumps or aggregations in the natural forest; these species have been successfully adapted to plantation cultivation. Other species, such as *Grevillea robusta,* which normally grow as scattered individuals, do not do well in plantations. *Grevillea* grew rapidly, in cultivation, for 10–12 years, then declined in growth despite thinning. Regeneration of the species by seed in the plantation was nil. The government officially labeled the plantations failures. In contrast, growth and regeneration of *Araucaria* in plantations were excellent. Although the authors did not isolate any toxins, they suggested that a root exudate was a factor, and that the chemical inhibition was an ecological factor of significance in maintaining dispersal of *Grevillea* individuals in the forest. Such dispersal may be advantageous in reducing damage from pathogens and herbivores (*26*); however they did not document any differences in the species of pathogens and herbivores that attack *Grevillea* on the one hand, *Araucaria* on the other. If they are the same for both trees or the intensity of attack is equal, the advantage of dispersion over aggregation is not obvious, and the significance of the biochemical interaction is even less obvious.

Few researchers have concerned themselves with the role of chemicals in directing community succession. In the Piedmont area of North Carolina, Keever (*27*) began her work on succession in the hope of finding a chemical basis. However, she concluded that succession there was mainly directed by growth form of the plants involved (annual, biennial, perennial), time of germination, amount of shade cast, or efficiency of seed dispersal. She found little or no evidence for chemical control.

Wilson and Rice (*28*) and Olmstead and Rice (*29*), however, have reported that plant byproducts may influence succession in Oklahoma. They found that aqueous extracts of one pioneer weed, *Helianthus annuus*, were toxic to germination and growth of that species and of associated weed species. Two of the toxins involved were chlorogenic and isochlorogenic acid. In laboratory bioassays, these compounds were toxic to 12-day-old seedlings of weeds such as *Amaranthus retroflexus* but not to plants of the next successional stage, such as *Aristida oligantha* (Table II). Field soils in weed communities were eluted, and extracts were isolated by paper chromatography. The majority of the separates proved toxic to *Amaranthus retroflexus* germination, but their identity was not determined, so it was not possible to say that chlorogenic acid and isochlorogenic acid were present in natural soil. However, since *Amaranthus retroflexus* is not native to Oklahoma, it has not evolved with the local flora and vegetation. How significant, then, are the chemical interactions revealed here to the composition and dynamics of more "natural" communities?

The Producer–Herbivore Level

For a given herbivore, all species of plants are not equally palatable. Many species are rejected totally, some are eaten preferentially, and others are eaten only when preferential species are absent. Grazing selectivity is easy to observe in large herbivores, but it is less obvious— though just as common—in small herbivores such as insects. The attainment of nonpalatability would confer major selective advantage to a plant species, and breeding programs directed to this end have major agricultural and economic implications. It is quite likely that palatability depends upon the quality and quantity of certain metabolic byproducts. For example, Gustafsson and Gadd (*30*) compared thrip damage on two varieties of a lupine species, one with a high alkaloid content, the other with low content, and reported that almost all thrips in a mixed-field planting were on the low alkaloid variety.

In lengthy reviews, Brower and Brower (*31*) and Ehrlich and Raven (*32*) summarized the food preferences of butterfly groups throughout the world. They concluded that many taxonomic groups feed exclusively on one to several families of flowering plants, and that: ". . . secondary plant substances play the leading role in determining patterns of utiliza-

Table II. Effect of Chlorogenic Acid on Seedling Weight of a Weed Species (*Amaranthus*) and an Annual Grass (*Aristida*) [a]

	Chlorogenic Acid, ppm					
	0	*0.029*	*0.289*	*2.89*	*28.9*	*289*
Amaranthus retroflexus	84.5	72.5	72.7	71.9	70.2	36.1
Aristida oligantha	32.1	32.8	30.9	31.1	36.1	31.9

[a] Seedlings were exposed for 12 days, then dry weight (mg) noted. Figures underlined differ from the control at the 5% significance level. Data from Olmstead and Rice (*29*).

tion. This seems true not only for butterflies but for all phytophagous groups and also for those parasitic on plants. In this context, the irregular distribution in plants of such chemical compounds of unknown physiological function as alkaloids, quinones, essential oils (including terpenoids), glycosides (including cyanogenic substances and saponins), flavonoids, and even raphides (needlelike calcium oxalate crystals) is immediately explicable."

It is doubtful that the data available justify quite such a sweeping statement. First, although the physiological functions of many compounds they mention are indeed unknown, it may not be fair to take them out of the context of metabolic pathways. They may be intermediates in the synthesis of pigments, hormones, or other compounds of known function. Conflicting reports on their rate of turnover exist. Second, the reviewers did not correlate plant chemistry specifically with feeding preference; they simply assumed that taxonomically (basically that means morphologically) related plants would be similar in their chemical composition. In a very simple, direct way, the work of Brower (below) indicates that this assumption cannot be made. Third, we still need more cause-and-effect evidence for the relationship between plant chemistry and feeding preference. Much research understandably stops at the correlation level: feeding activity is associated with differences in plant chemistry. However, such correlations leave other factors, which might be more critical in determining feeding preferences, unexamined. One of the few ecologists who pursues the correlations to a cause-and-effect level, and who has shown the importance of herbivory on community structure, is Janzen (26, 33, 34).

Brower (35, 36) has also accumulated evidence of a cause-and-effect relationship which illustrates the selective advantage of restricted feeding in a food chain. Monarch butterflies, common in tropical and subtropical areas, induce vomiting in birds which prey on them. Avoidance of the butterfly is soon learned by the birds. Apparently, vomiting is caused by large amounts of cardiac glycosides in the butterfly. Brower has demonstrated that these glycosides are not formed *de novo* by the butterfly but must be ingested by larvae from food plants.

Like other groups of unpalatable butterflies, the monarchs feed exclusively on a narrow taxonomic range of plants: the Asclepiadaceae (milkweed family) in this case. In Trinidad, Brower noted that the principal monarch larval food plant was *Asclepias curassavica*, a plant which contains a large amount and variety of cardiac glycosides. Larvae raised on this species in the laboratory contained 10 identifiable cardiac glycosides and, when fed to starved jays, caused vomiting. A minor food plant in Trinidad is another species of Asclepiadaceae, *Gonolobus rostratus*. This plant contains no cardiac glycosides, and larvae raised on this plant proved palatable to the test birds. Thus, palatability was caused solely by larval food plants, but because all the monarch butterflies look alike, birds avoid them all.

Why did the larvae feed mainly on the plant with high levels of cardiac glycosides? A second experiment, conducted in Florida, may have provided the answer. As diagrammed in Table III, two species of *Asclepias* serve as food plants for monarchs in that area, one with glycosides, one without. Feeding experiments were conducted, similar to those in Trinidad, and again palatability of the butterfly was solely the result of larval food plant. When Brower checked the egg-laying preference of the butterfly, he found that 93% of all eggs counted in nature had been laid on the glycoside-rich *Asclepias* species. What factor induced the females to oviposit on that species was not reported, but it is clear that the cycle of nonpalatability will be maintained by selective egg-laying behavior.

Feeny and Bostock (37) have found a relationship between timing of an insect life cycle and plant palatability. Larvae of the winter moth *Operophtera brumata* feed in spring on young leaves of the deciduous oak *Quercus robur*. The larvae are apparently intolerant of high tannin content in leaves, and the authors found that tannin content was minimal

Table III.   Plant Poisons in a Food Chain[a]

Trinidad		*Florida*	
Asclepias curassavica (*with cardiac glycosides*)	Gonolobus rostratus	A. humistrata (glycosides)	A. tuberosa
↓	↓	↓	↓
Monarch larvae (glycosides)	Monarch larvae	93% of all Monarch eggs	7% of all eggs
↓	↓	↓	↓
Monarch butterfly (glycosides)	Monarch butterfly	Larvae (glycosides)	Larvae
↓	↓	↓	↓
Induces vomiting in birds	No vomiting	Butterfly (glycosides)	Butterfly
		↓	↓
		Vomiting	No vomiting

[a] Data from Brower (*35*).

in spring. In April, when leaves first appear, tannin content is 0.5% (dry weight basis); by July it is 2%; by the end of September it reaches 5%. Feeny has speculated (*38*) that ". . . larvae of the winter moth will not mature satisfactorily on oak leaves 2 weeks older than those on which the larvae normally feed. If they hatch too early, they starve before the leaves appear; if they hatch too late, they are defeated by the tannins . . ." In some species (*a.g., Quercus lobata* of California), the deciduous habit may be an adaptation for avoidance of year-long herbivory rather than for avoidance of cold or drought.

Some herbivores increase the population size of their food plants, and pollinating insects are an example. Some pollinators are very selective in their flower choices, and perhaps the most complex interactions are between orchids and their pollinators. A few have flowers in the shape of female insects, and males attempt to copulate with them, resulting in pollination (*39*). Chemical scents play a major role, according to Dodson (*40*). He has shown that orchid flowers emit very specific scents produced by different ratios of terpenes and other aromatic hydrocarbons of low molecular weight (pinenes, cineoles, methyl salicylate). By placing these substances alone or in mixtures on blotter paper in nature and observing attraction of pollinators, he was able to conclude that combinations were discernable by the insects. For example, cineole and benzyl acetate mixed acted as a repellent for some species of pollinators, and modified the attraction potential of the total fragrance for others. Cineole or benzyl acetate alone had much less of a discriminating effect.

The most sophisticated and specific chemical interaction between plants and herbivores may involve hormones. Feeding preferences in some cases may be related to hormonal control rather than simple palatability. Ferns, for example, are generally less extensively eaten by insects than are flowering plants, and it may be no mere correlation that ferns evolved with the insects, considerably earlier than the flowering plants. Soo Hoo and Fraenkel (41) commented that larvae of the southern army worm reject ferns in general, and these authors performed some preliminary feeding experiments with ground pieces or water extracts of Boston fern (*Nephrolepis exaltata*). Shortly after, Kaplanis *et al.* (42) extracted two major molting hormones from pinnae of bracken fern (*Pteridium aquilinum*): α-ecdysone and 20-hydroxyecdysone (= β-ecdysone). Ecdysones form a class of compounds similar in structure to cholesterol; they are ordinarily synthesized by the prothoracic gland of larvae, and they promote developmental reactions, such as pupation. However, Kaplanis cautioned: ". . . we do not have information on either the significance or function of these steroids in plants. Perhaps . . . these substances . . . interfere with the growth processes of insect predators." His statement can still stand today.

As reviewed by Williams (43), ecdysone has been isolated from more than 10 species of conifers, 20 ferns, and 30 flowering plants (out of 1000 species surveyed). A total of 28 different plant ecdysones are known, the most ubiquitous being β-ecdysone. The ecological significance of β-ecdysone in plants is unclear. It is not toxic when orally ingested (as feeding larvae would obtain it from a food plant), but there is some evidence that it could be a feeding deterrent in concentrations as low as 1 ppb. Perhaps it serves as a steroid base for other compounds once it is in an insect's metabolic system.

Another developmental hormone is the juvenile hormone, which predominates early in larval life; later ecdysone predominates. It is a methyl ester of the epoxide of a fatty acid derivative, and there is some evidence that its structure differs in different groups of insects. By a series of coincidences, it was discovered that certain paper toweling prevented the European bug, *Pyrrhocoris apterus*, from developing into sexually mature adults. Instead, an extra one or two larval molts ensued, and all eventually died without being able to complete metamorphosis. The juvenility factor was traced to particular conifers used in American paper pulp, mainly *Abies balsamea, Tsuga canadensis, Taxus brevifolia*, and *Larix laricina*. The active principle was isolated and characterized. It has a structure similar to that of the juvenile hormone, and has been named juvabione. It proved to be effective on only one family of insects, the Pyrrhocoridae. Williams (*43*), who has summarized the story above, asked: "Have the plants in question undertaken these exorbitant syntheses just for fun? I think not. Present indications are that certain plants and more particularly the ferns and evergreen trees have gone in for an incredibly sophisticated self-defense against insect predation . . ."

However, the pyrrhocorid story certainly fails to justify such a hypothesis. *Pyrrhocoris apterus* is a native of Europe, and the only plants which produce the (very specific) juvabione are natives of North America. The two simply don't occur together. Further, the bug and all members of its family feed by sucking the juices of weak herbs; they are not known feeders of any tree species. What ecological significance is there in the pyrrhocorid story?

Plant substances are said to enhance some insect hormones, to the advantage of the insect. Bedard *et al.* (*44*) have described how the western pine beetle (*Dendroctonus brevicomis*) uses its host pine trees (*Pinus ponderosa* and *P. coulteri*) to enhance the drawing power of its sex attractant, exobrevicomin. When ready to mate, both sexes emit the attractant. Bedard found the attractant's power (in terms of numbers of insects attracted) was doubled when mixed with myrcene, a normal constituent of pine wood. Myrcene alone was not attractive. Myrcene, however, is not restricted to pine; we have seen earlier (*10*) that it is consistently found in spruce needles, and in general it is not characteristic of any single group of plants. Since the western pine beetle feeds only on pine, of what real ecological significance is Bedard's report of the enhancement of its hormone by myrcene? Why isn't a more specific constituent of pine wood involved? Perhaps one is, but research has not yet revealed it. Apart from Brower's work with the monarchs, we have not examined the rich area of herbivore–predator interactions.

Conclusions

Biochemical interactions between organisms do occur, and a more detailed review would document that conclusion abundantly, but how ecologically important are these interactions? What sometimes appears to be lacking in the recent literature is an appraisal of that question. The research is often incomplete.

Before ecological significance can be assigned to an interaction, a series of steps should be followed—in the manner Koch's postulates are followed to prove a causal relationship between a microbe and a disease. The first step involves considerable observation—a correlation must be documented. For example, negative association between two species of plants must be shown, or the selective feeding habits of a larva must be demonstrated. The correlation should be consistently apparent. A second step is experimentation. The correlation must be proved to be cause and effect. What factors maintain the correlation? If a chemical is involved, what is its identity and how does it affect the species involved? Much of this work can be done in the laboratory, but laboratory conditions should attempt to imitate field conditions. A third step returns to the field situation. Do the factors discovered in the laboratory operate in nature? Can the compounds be detected, and in what concentration? Can they remain viable in the soil system for long periods?

The pitfalls in carrying a suspected interaction through all three steps are numerous and well illustrated in the literature. Webb et al. (45), for example, checked into the negative association between a native Australian shrub and some introduced, annual weeds. They found that ground leaves of the shrub were indeed toxic to the introduced annuals, but that they were also toxic to native herbs, even to herbs which characteristically grew beneath the shrub. They concluded that ". . . this toxicity is ecologically irrelevant," and let us hope that the days of using tomatoes as test organisms for the inhibitory quality of desert shrub extracts are over (46); bioassays must have some ecological relevance. Carrying experiments to the field is perhaps the most difficult step. Muller and del Moral (47) made a fine attempt, but realized that the amount of inhibitor present in nature was less than that used to induce inhibition in the laboratory, and Bartholomew (22) pointed out the importance of other factors, such as grazing. Bonner (48) had to abandon his study when he discovered that an inhibitor active in sterile sand was rapidly broken down in normal, bacteria-rich soil.

In a recent paper, Whittaker (49) philosophically concluded that stability and diversity in communities can in large measure be caused by biochemical interactions. On the one hand, the interactions permit diversity by limiting competition between species. In effect, species are restricted to a smaller portion of the habitat, thus permitting more species to fit in. On the other hand, the interactions enhance stability in community composition by making it difficult for invaders to penetrate. In an evolutionary, rather than ecological, sense, Whittaker believed that chemical interactions favor diversity, because of ". . . virtually unlimited potentialities for the addition of different species with different interactions." However, in light of my brief review, I suggest that such broad conclusions be regarded as tenuous hypotheses for the moment, until the ecological significance of many of the reported biochemical interactions is proved.

Literature Cited

1. Ehrenfeld, D. W., "Biological Conservation," Holt Rinehart and Winston, San Francisco, Calif., 1970.
2. Clements, F. E., "Plant Succession," Publication 242, Carnegie Institute, Washington, D. C., 1970.
3. Sondheimer, E., Simeone, J. B., Eds., "Chemical Ecology," Academic, New York, 1970.
4. Eyre, S. R., "Vegetation and Soils," Aldine, Chicago, Ill., 1963.
5. Melin, E., Nilsson, H., *Svensk Bot. Tidsk.* (1955) **49**, 119.
6. Scott, G. D., "Plant Symbiosis," St. Martin's Press, New York, 1969.
7. Woods, F. W., Brock, K., *Ecology* (1964) **45**, 886.
8. Carlisle, A., Brown, A. H. F., White, E. J., *J. Ecol.* (1966) **54**, 87.
9. Tukey, H. B., *Bull. Torrey Bot. Club* (1966) **93**, 385.
10. von Rudloff, E., *Can. J. Bot.* (1967) **45**, 891.
11. Went, F. W., *Nature (London)* (1960) **187**, 641.
12. Booth, W. E., *Amer. J. Bot.* (1941) **28**, 415.
13. Rice, E. L., *Ecology* (1964) **45**, 824.
14. Rice, E. L., *Physiol. Plant.* (1965) **18**, 255.
15. Blum, U., Rice, E. L., *Bull. Torrey Bot. Club* (1969) **96**, 531.
16. Robinson, T., "The Organic Constituents of Higher Plants," 2nd ed, Burgess, Minneapolis, Minn., 1967.
17. Wang, T. S. C., Yang, T., Chuang, T., *Soil Sci.* (1967) **103**, 239.
18. Patrick, Z. A., Koch, L. W., *Can. J. Bot.* (1958) **36**, 621.
19. Brian, P. W., *Annu. Rev. Plant Physiol.* (1957) **8**, 413.
20. Rennerfelt, E., Nacht, G., *Svensk Bot. Tidsk.* (1955) **49**, 332.
21. Muller, C. H., *Bull. Torrey Bot. Club* (1966) **93**, 332.
22. Bartholomew, B., *Science* (1970) **170**, 1210.
23. Muller, C. H., *Vegetatio* (1969) **18**, 348.
24. Brown, R. T., *Ecology* (1967) **48**, 542.
25. Webb, L. J., Tracey, J. G., Haydock, K. P., *J. Appl. Ecol.* (1967) **4**, 13.
26. Janzen, D. H., *Ecology* (1972) **53**, 350.
27. Keever, C., *Ecol. Monogr.* (1950) **20**, 229.
28. Wilson, R. E., Rice, E. L., *Bull. Torrey Bot. Club* (1968) **95**, 432.
29. Olmsted, C. E., Rice, E. L., *Southwest. Nat.* (1970) **15**, 165.
30. Gustafsson, A., Gadd, I., *Hereditas* (1965) **53**, 15.
31. Brower, L. P., Brower, J., *Zoologica* (1964) **49**, 137.
32. Ehrlich, P. R., Raven, P. H., *Evolution* (1965) **18**, 586.
33. Janzen, D. H., *Evolution* (1969) **12**, 1.
34. Janzen, D. H., *Amer. Nat.* (1970) **104**, 501.
35. Brower, L. P., in "Biochemical Coevolution," pp. 69–82, Chambers, K. L., Ed., Oregon State University Press, Corvallis, Ore., 1968.
36. Brower, L. P., Brower, J., Corvino, J., *Proc. Nat. Acad. Sci. U. S.* (1967) **57**, 893.
37. Feeny, P. P., Bostock, H., *Phytochemistry* (1968) **7**, 871.
38. Ehrlich, P. R., in ref. 35, pp. 1–11.
39. Weier, T. E., Stocking, C. R., Barbour, M. G., "Botany," 4th ed, Wiley, New York, 1970.
40. Dodson, C. H., in Ref. 35, pp. 83–107.
41. Soo Hoo, C. F., Fraenkel, G., *Entomol. Soc. Amer. Ann.* (1964) **57**, 788.
42. Kaplanis, J. N., Thompson, M. J., Robbins, W. E., Bryce, B. M., *Science* (1967) **57**, 1436.
43. Williams, C. M., in "Chemical Ecology," pp. 103–132, Sondheimer, E., Simeone, J. B., Eds., Academic, New York, 1970.
44. Bedard, W. D., Tilden, P. E., Wood, D. L., Silverstein, R. M., Brownlee, R. G., Rodin, J. O., *Science* (1969) **164**, 1284.
45. Webb, L. J., Tracey, J. G., Haydock, K. P., *Aust. J. Sci.* (1961) **24**, 244.

46. Bennett, E. L., Bonner, J., *Amer. J. Bot.* (1953) **40**, 29.
47. Muller, C. H., del Moral, R., *Bull. Torrey Bot. Club* (1966) **93**, 130.
48. Bonner, J., *Bot. Rev.* (1950) **16**, 51.
49. Whittaker, R. H., in "Diversity and Stability in Ecological Systems," *Brookhaven Symp. Biol.* (1970) **22**, 178.

RECEIVED September 23, 1971.

9

Oxidant-Induced Community Change in a Mixed Conifer Forest

PAUL L. MILLER[1]

Pacific Southwest Forest and Range Experiment Station, Forest Service, U. S. Department of Agriculture, Berkeley, Calif.

Trees of the ponderosa pine-sugar pine-fir forest type on the San Bernardino National Forest in southern California are exposed to heavy chronic photochemical oxidant air pollution. The relative numbers, age-composition, and spatial distribution of coniferous trees in this forest type were determined. Total mortality of ponderosa pines was 8% during a two-year period and 10% during four years in a separate sample. Continuous records of oxidant exposure during a five-year period helped to relate dosage to observed damage. Possible physical and biological changes in this forest type are suggested, and questions of importance to forest management are identified.

Photochemical oxidant air pollution—chiefly ozone—was first identified in 1962 as the agent responsible for the slow decline and death of ponderosa pine (*Pinus ponderosa* Laws.) trees in southern California (*1*). Work on identifying this source of damage can be traced to the mid-1950's; it was described as "chlorotic decline" (*2*).

Ponderosa pine is one of the five major species in the ponderosa pine-sugar pine-fir forest cover type (*3*) on the San Bernardino National Forest in southern California. The other species in this type are sugar pine (*P. lambertiana* Dougl.), white fir (*Abies concolor* Lindl. & Gord.), incense cedar (*Libocedrus decurrens* Torr.), and California black oak (*Quercus Kelloggii* Newb.) (*3*). This cover type—sometimes called "the mixed conifer type"—occupies wide areas of the western Sierra Nevada and the mountain ranges in southern California from 3000 to 6000 feet

[1] Located at Riverside, Calif. 92507.

elevation (3). Above 6000 feet, Jeffrey pine (*Pinus Jeffreyi* Grev. & Balf.) replaces ponderosa pine.

Several of the most numerous understory and herb layer plants on sunny, dry sites of the study area are: canyon live oak (*Quercus chrysolepis* Liebm.), pink-bract manzanita (*Arctostaphylos Pringlei* Parry var. *drupacea* Parry), deerbrush [*Ceanothus integerrimus* var. *puberlus* (Green) Abrams], bracken fern [*Pteris aquilinum* (L.) Kuhn var. *lanuginosum* (Bong.)], cheatgrass (*Bromus tectorum* L.), and California brome (*Bromus carinatus* H. & A.). Plants typical of shady, moist sites are: mountain dogwood (*Cornus nuttallii* Aud.), willow (*Salix lasiandra* Benth. var. *Abramsii* Ball.), Sierra currant (*Ribes nevadense* Kell.), thimbleberry (*Rubus parviflorus* Nutt.), and lupine [*Lupinus polyphyllus* Lindl. ssp. *bernardinus* (Abrams) Munz.].

Sugar pine, incense cedar, and black oak have suffered only slight damage from chronic oxidant exposure. White fir has suffered slight damage, but occasional trees are severely damaged. As yet, there has been no mortality among these three species which can be attributed to oxidant damage. Jeffrey pine resembles ponderosa in sensitivity to air pollution damage.

In 1969 an aerial photo survey by the U. S. Forest Service of the San Bernardino National Forest showed that 1.3 million ponderosa or Jeffrey pines (12 inches or larger, diameter at breast height) on more than 100,000 acres were affected to some degree (4).

A recent ground survey covering limited portions of California has identified slight oxidant damage to ponderosa pine, particularly in the Sierra Nevada foothills east of Fresno (5). The prospect of continued damage in southern California and new damage in other areas has generated concern about the total effect on all plant and animal species associated with the ponderosa pine-sugar pine-fir type.

Most of the work to date has been directed at assessing the impact of ozone on the vegetative growth phases of ponderosa pine. There are no published studies that have included its conifer or hardwood associates or understory vegetation.

This paper describes the present stand composition, degree of injury, and mortality in ponderosa pine in relation to the concentrations of oxidant air pollution in a heavily damaged area and points out some possible physical and biological factors associated with oxidant-induced changes in community composition.

The Study Area

The study area was a 575-acre block on undulating ridgetop and generally north-facing slopes in the northwest section of the San Bernardino National Forest. The undulating ridgetop represents the abrupt southern boundary of the coniferous forest, where there is a sharp transition into the woodland chaparral characterized by canyon live oak and big cone Douglas-fir (*Pseudotsuga macrocarpa* Mayn.) (6).

The southern boundary overlooks the urban basin below and is subjected first to the polluted air which is convected over the crest almost daily during spring, summer, and fall (7). The elevation at the southern one-third of the plot is gently rolling at 5600 ft elevation, but northward the terrain changes into gently sloping ridges and relatively steep ravines, culminated at the northern end by an intermittent stream at about 5400 ft. Beyond the northern boundary of the plot, the coniferous forest continues for about 4 miles where it adjoins a steep chaparral zone overlooking the Mojave Desert.

The cactus granite formation is the dominant parent material in the study area. This formation which is largely a light-colored quartz monzonite of the Mesozoic age (8) is found in occasional outcrops on the ridgetop and north-facing slopes above 5400 ft. The soil is typically deep and well developed most closely resembling the Shaver coarse sandy loam.

From 1943 through 1971 the precipitation at the Lake Arrowhead Fire District station about 1 mile ENE of the study area averaged 40.04 inches (January-December). The standard deviation of 18.05 was exceeded five times below and five times above the mean. The 1870–1970 average estimated from isohyetals (San Bernardino County Flood Control Agency map) is between 35 and 40 inches. A dry trend continued without interruption from 1959 through 1964 with precipitation averaging 11.21 inches below the 1943–1971 average. Since 1964 the annual precipitation was: 1965, 67.19; 1966, 38.01; 1967, 55.87; 1968, 20.06; 1969, 98.54; 1970, 34.61; and 1971, 33.80.

The present uses of the land include a few leased summer cabin sites, and an improved public campground in the southwest corner. Compared with the intense use of nearby lands under private ownership, this area is lightly used.

During the 1860's, the study area was heavily logged for the first time, and possibly a second cutting occurred during the 1890's. The forest composition in that virgin stand is not known, but early photographs and other records suggest that ponderosa and sugar pine were the species harvested in greatest abundance. The amount of white fir in the unlogged stand is not definitely known, but this species was not considered of great timber value. The uses of incense cedar may also have been limited because of the common occurrence of decay in the larger sized stems (9).

A major wildfire in August 1911 may have burned a small strip along the western boundary of the area. In 1956 the extreme southern boundary of the area may have received damage from a fire burning up from the woodland chaparral.

Methods

Survey Procedures. Eight survey strips were laid out running east-west at nearly equal distant intervals (crossing drainages at right angles). Each strip was 66 ft wide, and the lengths varied from 0.3 to 1.4 miles. An observer walked the center line and recorded the numbers within 33 ft on the right and left of ponderosa pine, sugar pine, white fir, and incense cedar in four size classes: saplings, 3.01 ft tall to 3.99 inches dbh (diameter at breast height); poles, 4.00 to 11.99 inches dbh; standard, 12.00 to 23.99 inches dbh; and veteran, 24.00 inches dbh or larger. The numbers of seedlings less than 3.00 ft tall were determined within the boundaries of a 6.6 sq ft frame that was placed on the center line every 132 ft. A total of 278 milacre plots were studied. The total acres observed in the eight survey strips were 53.4 or about 9% of the total 575 acres. This sample size was considered adequate to provide a reliable estimate of species composition and size distribution.

Each ponderosa pine 4.00 inches dbh or larger was examined and assigned a value to describe the degree of oxidant injury. This score system for pine was a slight modification of a method used previously with aerial photographic techniques to detect and evaluate oxidant injury (4):

Characteristic	*Score*
Needle retention (number of years retained)	
upper crown	0–6
lower crown	0–6
Needle condition (one score value given to each annual whorl)	
upper crown	
green	4
chlorotic mottle	2
uniform yellow or necrosis	0
lower crown	
Green	4
chlorotic mottle	2
uniform yellow or necrosis	0
Needle length (upper and lower crown)	
average expected length	1
less than expected length	0
Branch mortality (lower crown)	
normal mortality	1
pronounced mortality	0

Binoculars were used routinely to determine needle condition in the upper tree crown. Trees were categorized according to the total score value for each as: 0, dead; 1–8, very severe injury; 9–14, severe injury; 15–21, moderate injury; 22–28, slight injury; 29–35, very slight injury; and 36–62, no visible symptoms.

On one survey strip, 160 ponderosa pines were tagged and assigned score values in April 1969. The same trees were re-evaluated in May 1971 to determine the change in degree of oxidant injury and the number of deaths.

Oxidant Air Pollution Monitoring. Oxidant air pollution was recorded continuously from April to November for five years with a Mast model 724-2 ozone meter and a strip chart recorder housed in a weatherproof enclosure. The permanent station was at Rim Forest (5640 ft elevation) about two-fifths of a mile southwest of the study area. The ozone meters were calibrated every three to four weeks in the laboratory against buffered 2% KI. The calibration factor included a positive correction for the altitude difference of 4600 ft between the laboratory where calibration was done and the sample site.

Results

Species and Age Composition in Relation to Site. Combining all sites on the study area, the species composition in the understory (seedlings up through poles 11.99 inches dbh) is ponderosa pine, 22.2%; incense cedar, 48.6%; white fir, 22.8%; and sugar pine, 6.3%. In the overstory (trees larger than 12.00 inches dbh) it is ponderosa, 49.6%; incense cedar, 22.7%; white fir, 19.7%; and sugar pine, 8.0%. Table I shows the actual numbers in each size class.

Black oak was not included in the survey initially, but a separate sample of oaks and conifers 4.00 inches dbh or larger was obtained in a 100 × 550 ft plot on the ridgetop where it comprised 11.0% of the stand. In this sample, the conifer composition was: ponderosa pine, 60.4%; incense cedar, 20.6%; white fir, 5.8%; and sugar pine, 2.2%.

Ponderosa pine was most abundant at the upper end of the study area on the rounded ridge crest overlooking the urban basin to the south. White fir (saplings and poles) became more numerous on the various microaspects of the generally north-facing slope. Incense cedar and sugar pine were more uniformly distributed over the area.

This information partially suggests the kind of site where each species has the greatest competitive advantage over its companion conifers, California black oak, and understory shrubs. The possible influences of logging and its associated seedbed modifications as well as old wildfires must be weighed in relation to site factors as determinants of the present stand composition. The detailed age and species composition data in

Table I.   Tree Species and Size Composition on a Study Site Affected by
Oxidant Air Pollution[a]

Tree Size Class	Ponderosa Pine	Incense Cedar	White Fir	Sugar Pine
	Number/Acre			
Understory				
Seedlings (up to 3.00 ft tall)	1057	2381	1043	302
Saplings (more than 3.01 ft tall, less than 3.99 inches dbh)	33	33	57	10
Poles (4.00 to 11.99 inches (dbh)	21	12	38	3
Percent:	22.2	48.6	22.8	6.3
Overstory				
Standard (12.00 to 23.99 inches dbh)	18	9	8	3
Veteran (24 inches dbh and larger)	12	5	4	2
Percent:	49.6	22.7	19.7	8.0

[a] Trees from 575-acre study area, San Bernadino National Forest, Calif.

Table I cannot yet show the imprint of changes induced by oxidant air
pollution because there is no earlier information to compare it with. This
information does permit some speculations about future stand composition
however.

Condition of Living Ponderosa Pines in 1969. Detailed inspection
of ponderosa pines in the three largest size classes was completed on
each of eight sample strips of which three represented the ridge crest
and five represented various site aspects of the north-facing slope. A
total of 2857 trees were observed, of which 1219 were poles, 1004 standards, and 634 veterans. No significant differences in the amount of oxidant
injury observed could be related to tree size. Stark *et al.* (*10*) also concluded that the degree of oxidant injury was not related to tree height
or diameter in this same vicinity. In the larger sample combining all tree
sizes on eight sample strips, 16.1% had slight, 33.3% moderate, 31.2%
severe, and 19.4% very severe injury.

Further inspection of the tree condition on each sample strip clearly
indicated a trend of increased injury on the three ridge crest strips. This
finding emphasizes the importance of site in relation to the potential for
injury by chronic oxidant exposure. Trees on the more exposed, wind-
swept, drier site appear to suffer greater injury than those on the more
protected north-facing slopes. Under these circumstances, the damage
might be characterized as a deterioration at the forest boundary. Drought
was shown to affect the annual terminal growth of both damaged and

relatively undamaged ponderosa pines, but only the undamaged trees responded after years with increased precipitation. The damaged trees continued to decline in terminal growth and vigor (2). The role of soil moisture availability in influencing the severity of oxidant damage is not clearly understood.

Increase of Damage to Ponderosa Pines from 1969 to 1971. Ponderosa pines larger than 4 inches dbh were selected at random on a sample line on the upper one-third of the study area or ridge crest where elevation ranged from 5520 to 5720 ft. This group of 160 trees was first observed in April 1969, when each tree was assigned a score value for severity of oxidant damage. The same trees were re-evaluated in May 1971. The mean score value for the 160 trees dropped from 12.5 to 11.3, a deterioration which proved statistically significant at the 1% confidence level in the paired "T" test. Both means remain within the "severe injury" category. The greatest increase in injury was among those trees initially classed in the very slight or slight injury categories (Table II). The

Table II.   Changes in 160 Ponderosa Pine Trees during Exposure to Oxidant Air Pollution from 1969 to 1971 [a]

Tree Condition and Score Range	1969		1971	
	No.	*%*	*No.*	*%*
Dead (0)	0	0	13	8.1
Very severe (1–8)	62	38.8	51	31.9
Severe (9–14)	46	28.7	53	33.1
Moderate (15–21)	25	15.6	32	20.0
Slight (22–28)	27	16.9	11	6.9

[a] Drop in average tree injury score from 12.5 to 11.3 is statistically significant at the 1% level.

mortality during this period was 8%: 11 trees in the very severe category, and two trees in the severe injury category. A smaller sample of 40 ponderosa pines also located on the ridge crest was observed from 1968 to 1972. The mortality was 10% during this period, and there was a drop of 3.86 in damage score.

Bark beetles were responsible for the death of the weakened trees in almost all cases. Six miles west of the study area, Cobb and Stark (11) observed 24% mortality over a three-year period when 34 of 150 trees died. Bark beetles were again considered to be responsible for tree mortality.

Binocular inspection revealed evidence of a cone crop on just eight trees of the 160 tree sample during the two years as judged by remnants of cones on twigs, small cones that did not drop to the ground, or new female conelets. Recent observations along a gradient of decreasing oxidant exposure in the San Bernardino mountains have shown significantly greater frequency of cone-bearing trees in the low exposure area (*12*).

The rate at which trees deteriorate before bark beetle infestation varies widely. Particularly in the very severe and severe injury categories, some trees of the 160-tree sample showed slight improvement, and some remained in the same condition after two years. The oxidant air pollution levels remained about the same from 1968 to 1972. This condition emphasizes the importance of the other physical and biological factors of the environment in triggering tree mortality.

Figure 1.   Change in a ponderosa pine during 10 years of chronic exposure to photochemical oxidant air pollution on the San Bernardino National Forest, southern California

In another observation of the rate of tree decline, 20 ponderosa pines were observed and photographed in 1961. In 1969 seven of the trees remained about the same even though some were in poor condition to start. Another seven trees had deteriorated considerably (Figure 1), and four more had died. The remaining two had been cut down. Observation of larger numbers of trees over a longer period and broader area will be necessary to characterize fully the dynamics of tree decline and death.

Annual Exposure to Oxidant Concentrations. Air monitoring was not done during winter because conditions then result in much less confinement of air pollutants by the marine temperature inversion in the adjacent basin below the forest, less oxidant synthesis during shorter days, and less frequent transport of polluted air to the forest.

Total oxidant concentrations have remained fairly stable for five years. During May to September of each year, mean values for daily maxima (Figure 2) and the corresponding means for hours exceeding 0.10 ppm daily were:

Year	Mean Values (ppm)	Hours Exceeding 0.10 ppm Daily
1968	0.20	10.6
1969	0.18	9.5
1970	0.22	8.8
1971	0.22	7.9
1972	0.22	9.7

The averages of daily oxidant maxima for each month were the highest in May, June, July, and August in the mountains (Figure 2). The number of hours daily when oxidant concentrations exceeded 0.10 ppm (the standard in California above which oxidant constitutes a community air pollution problem) varied from 9.5 to 10.7 hours when five-year averages of May–August were compared. September averaged 6.1 hours above 0.10 ppm.

The most severe single daily maximum of 0.58 ppm at Rim Forest occurred in June 1970. This concentration exceeds all of the alert levels prescribed by nearby urban communities; for example, when oxidant concentrations exceed 0.27 ppm, school children are not permitted to exercise strenuously in the city of Riverside, Calif.

Discussion

Ponderosa pines 12.00 inches dbh or larger are significantly more numerous than any other species of this size in the study area. The predominance of ponderosa pine is most pronounced on the more exposed ridge crest site. The results of this study suggest that the average tree suffers severe damage and is deteriorating at an alarming rate. Tree mortality ranged from 8% during 1969 to 1971 in one sample to 10% from 1968 to 1972 in a second sample. Measurements of oxidants from 1968 to 1972 suggest that air quality had not improved in those years.

Perhaps the selective removal of ponderosa pine by air pollution would not be considered with alarm or regarded any differently from selective logging if there were assurance that the reproductive and vege-

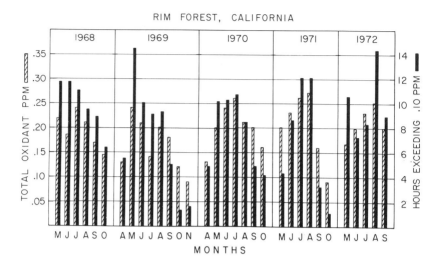

Figure 2. Total oxidant concentrations at Rim Forest (5640 ft), southern California, were high during May, June, July, and August, in the five years measured. Values of total oxidant are averages of daily maxima for a month. The number of hours in which total oxidant exceeded 10 ppm was also recorded for the five years.

tative growth of the remaining individuals could proceed normally. The continued exposure to oxidant air pollution raises many important questions about the reproductive and vegetative vigor of the conifer species, their ability to compete successfully with other associated vegetation, and to withstand diseases, insects, and extremes of the physical environment.

The present scarcity of data only allows limited speculation about the community changes expected to be induced by oxidant air pollution in the coniferous forest. An enormous amount of new information must be compiled for each important overstory and understory species in a life table format. This procedure identifies the relative importance of the various mortality factors which act upon each age or size class of each important species in the mixture from seedling to maturity.

Oxidant air pollution is one of several competing mortality factors which acts in all age classes, and it has already been shown to interact synergistically with another mortality factor—the pine bark beetle—to hasten death. Other interactions must be identified and evaluated. A complex predictive computer model will be required to handle such massive amounts of data and eventually quantify the important impacts of oxidant air pollution on this forest ecosystem.

The following discussion attempts to lay some of the groundwork for constructing life tables and preparing a conceptual model by examining some of the most pertinent literature.

Survival and Competition in Early Growth Stages. The selective death of ponderosa pine in a conifer mixture with sugar pine, white fir, and incense cedar is an incident which directly affects other conifer species in the community. The conifer species compete with each other and with broad-leaved tree and shrub species for available light, soil moisture, nutrients, and space throughout their life span.

The future composition of the forest will be determined to a large extent by the relative ability of conifers, hardwood trees, shrubs, grasses, and herbs to become established or to survive if already present in the new clearings formed where large ponderosa pines once stood. It is reasonable to assume that oxidant air pollution will continue to inflict considerable damage, particularly on ponderosa pine, including possibly the suppression of vigor of the more oxidant-tolerant individuals. The substantial shift of ponderosa pines from the category of "slight injury" to "moderate injury" (Table II) suggests that there may be no positive resistance to ozone injury or homeostatic condition. This situation may make this species even less successful as a competitor with other vegetation.

ESTABLISHMENT OF SEEDLINGS. Some work has been done on the establishment and survival of out-planted seedlings in the southern California mountains (13), but little is known about natural regeneration. Some limited generalizations can be made from studies of natural regeneration made in the Sierra Nevada. Recently disturbed mineral soil is the best seedling substrate for all of the conifers in this forest cover type (14). White fir (15) and sugar pine (16) also become established on a litter-covered surface. White fir is not encouraged by the environmental conditions in clearings (17). In the first stages of seedling development, incense cedar survives best under partial shade (14).

Under environmental conditions in the Stanislaus National Forest, in central California, which may or may not be comparable with those in the southern California mountains, long-term observations of seedling regeneration indicated: ponderosa and sugar pines were favored by removal of the overstory, understory, and ground competition; white fir was favored by a light overstory which prevented frost damage (18). In that study, incense cedar was selectively removed by cutworms (Noctuidae), which made it difficult to assess the comparative effect of the physical environment on survival.

If air pollution effects could be ignored, seedling and sapling ponderosa pines appear to be the most successful candidates for survival in the new clearings in the study area. Sugar pine may be the second most successful species in ability to be established. The clearings which are developing on the study site would be colder at night because of greater heat re-radiation to the open sky above, resulting in greater danger of

freezing injury to the seedlings there. The order of increasing susceptibility to freezing injury is incense cedar, sugar pine, and white fir (19).

COMPETITION. Brush can be a severe problem in the establishment
of sugar pine seedlings (20) unless the site is prepared (21). Sugar pine
is not as shade-tolerant as white fir or incense cedar and, if it falls behind
white fir in particular in the race for dominance, it will decline in growth
(14). Although incense cedar can endure heavy shade in the seedling
stage, it requires more light in later stages (22).

White fir is a formidable competitor in mixed conifer stands because
heavy litter, brush, and ground cover favor it more than pines (14). In
northeastern California, a conversion of a 50:50 ponderosa pine-white fir
pole stand to nearly 100% fir was described as a result of extensive mortality of pine from bark beetle attack.

The foregoing example and the results of this study in which most
of the smog-damaged ponderosa are eventually infested with bark beetles
and quickly killed show some similarity (11).

The lack of pine seed production on remaining sugar and ponderosa
pines in a cut-over area on the Stanislaus National Forest coupled with
shade from competing vegetation allowed white fir and incense cedar to
fill in the available spaces from 1923 to 1947, so that pines comprised
only 5% of the reproduction by 1947 (20).

All of this information suggests that the lower two-thirds of our study
area may shift to a greater proportion of white fir where the species already comprises a significant proportion of the understory. Incense cedar
is now present in greater numbers in the understory on the site compared
with white fir (Table I). Incense cedar may remain secondary to white
fir as these trees pass into overstory size classes because its height growth
is usually slower than associated species of comparable age (15). Because sugar pine will be faced with difficult competition and dwarf
mistletoe infection, it may not increase in numbers. This shift in stand
composition will be governed by the rate of ponderosa pine mortality.

On the upper one-third of the study area, which is a more wind-
swept and severe site, there is already some indication that white fir does
not grow well there. It is known that white fir is more subject to windthrow than ponderosa pine (14). Perhaps sugar pine and incense cedar
will make up a greater proportion of the future stand; however, if natural
regeneration is relied upon, the present supply of sugar pine seed trees
is limited to only three per acre. Both species may have difficulty becoming established on the more barren, dry sites.

California black oak is moderately abundant throughout the study
area (11% of the mixture in one sample including oak and four conifers).
It should be considered a candidate for occupying the new clearings,
especially on the exposed ridge crest. The existing acreages of black

oak woodland were formed after the early logging of mature conifers from the area (6). Subsequent fires destroyed young conifers in areas similar to the study area, but oak sprouted successfully after fire and became more dominant in a mixture with a few surviving conifers.

During the past century, the conifer forests of this mountain area have been logged and burned to the extent that they have been replaced by brush or woodland chaparral (6). The inability of the conifer forest to regenerate after these events may be an important indicator of what to expect on some sites after removal of the conifer forest dominated by ponderosa pine.

The competitive ability of shrub species, such as pink-bracted manzanita or deerbrush, and other understory plants, such as grasses and bracken fern, must be considered especially on some of the more barren, dry sites.

Harward and Treshow (24) have suggested that ozone could completely remove the most sensitive understory plants in the aspen zone in Utah; it is likely that sensitive species may have already been eliminated from the heavily damaged mixed conifer forest of our study site.

Under conditions where sulfur dioxide was the major pollutant vegetation was stripped away in layers, starting with the larger overstory species, and the numbers of species present nearest the source diminished considerably from the original array (25). The most probable resemblance to the foregoing situation in our study area is that the dominant ponderosa pines are being selectively removed by chronic oxidant exposure.

Relative Effects on Established Conifers. The relative oxidant sensitivity of white fir, incense cedar, and sugar pine under field conditions was not defined by observations of plots in this study. Controlled exposure of container-grown individuals to ozone showed that all three species received injury after exposure to 0.45 ppm, 12 hours daily for about three weeks. Repeated fumigation experiments with 42 replications of each series in each test have shown the order of increasing sensitivity to be sugar pine, incense cedar, white fir, and ponderosa pine (12). It is always difficult to translate this information directly to larger trees under field conditions, but it strongly suggests significant sensitivity, particularly of white fir.

Oxidant air pollution may be eliminating only the most sensitive ponderosa pines from the forest, but there is undoubtedly suppression of the photosynthetic activity (26) and subsequent growth of the remaining trees.

The shoot and needle length and number of needle whorls retained increased immediately on ponderosa saplings maintained in a carbon-filtered air environment compared with those provided with oxidant-polluted air in the San Bernardino mountains. Other conifer species have not been compared in this way, but growth suppression is an almost certain consequence. Immediate recovery of damaged trees can be expected if air pollution were substantially reduced.

Effects on Seed Production. Moderately and severely damaged ponderosa pines do not produce a cone crop when the more healthy individuals do. Although no quantitative data have been taken to substantiate this particular case, there is evidence that vigorous trees are much better seed producers than less vigorous individuals (27). Fowells and Schubert (27) observed during a 16-year period in California that the more vigorous dominant ponderosa pines produced more than 99% of the cones, and trees in all other classes produced only 1%. In the same study, ponderosa pines in the pole stage up to those trees 50 inches dbh produced considerably more cones than sugar pine but then declined in cone production earlier than sugar pine. White fir produced more cones in its early years than did ponderosa or sugar pines, but they declined in seed production at an earlier age. Ponderosa pine produces cones most abundantly when in the 25-to-50 inch dbh range. The removal of trees in the upper end of this size range constitutes the greatest loss in potential seed production.

The individual ponderosa pines and members of other species which are more tolerant to oxidant may produce cones, but perhaps fewer than in a clean air environment because chronic oxidant exposure decreases their vigor. Furthermore, it is questionable whether there will be a sufficient number of sound seed even though cones are bountiful. Feder (28) has shown inhibition of pollen germ tube growth of tobacco caused by ozone exposure.

The western gray squirrel (*Sciurus griseus anthonyi* Mearns), which has remained abundant in the area, actively cuts the developing cones and young twigs from the tree. Assuming that the remaining oxidant-tolerant ponderosa pines can produce cone crops, these survivors may be exploited more intensely by the squirrels in their search for food. The resultant damage could reduce future cone crops (29) and thus diminish the importance of these survivors as parents of new generations of more oxidant-tolerant trees.

Possible Predisposition to Injury. Stomatal behavior may be an important determinant of the amount of suppression of photosynthesis and resultant visible damage. Measurements of temperature, vapor pressure gradient, and total oxidant continuously during July and August in the conifer forest indicate that the maximum oxidant concentration occurs between 1600 and 1900 PST when both vapor pressure gradient and temperature are decreasing rapidly (7); in other words, the oxidant arrives with the cool, moist, marine air.

During the late afternoon when the vapor pressure gradient declines, ponderosa pine stomata may open wider, resulting in greater oxidant uptake and simultaneous depression of carbon dioxide fixation. Some knowledge of stomatal function would be useful to see if there is any relationship between intraspecific oxidant tolerance and ability to close stomates in the presence of elevated ozone concentrations. This mechanism is an inherited characteristic of an ozone-resistant onion variety which closes its stomates when exposed to ozone (*30*). It is not known if this mechanism is involved in conditioning interspecific tolerance or sensitivity of the important conifer species.

Influence on Host–Parasite Relationships. Cobb and Stark (*11*) have directed considerable attention to the increased incidence of attack of oxidant-injured ponderosa pines by bark beetles in the San Bernardino mountains. They suggest that ponderosa pine will nearly be eliminated from the mixed conifer forest if such attacks continue. Increased activity of other insect pests of ponderosa pine or associated conifers has not been observed.

Infection by dwarf mistletoe and true mistletoe of conifer hosts is commonplace in the San Bernardino and Angeles National Forests. There is no experimental evidence to define the ozone sensitivity of the aerial shoots of the mistletoes relative to the foliage of their conifer hosts. Cursory observations of dwarf mistletoe on pines suggest no injury to dwarf mistletoe shoots. The dwarf mistletoes derive their elaborated carbohydrates entirely from their host (*31*), and ozone probably depletes the stored carbohydrates of needle tissue (*26*) which may have been translocated to the parasite. The combined effect of these agents probably means greater stress on the host. On the other hand, true mistletoes manufacture their own carbohydrates (*31*) and may benefit the host if they are less sensitive to oxidant than the host tree.

Decreasing vigor of the aerial portions of the affected ponderosa pines has been associated with deterioration of the feeder root system (*2*). Extensive deterioration of the feeder rootlets may limit the uptake of nutrients and water. Root inhabiting fungi or saprophytic fungi may become more aggressive in the weakened rootlets, causing extensive decay. The common root pathogen [*Armillaria mellea* (Vahl. ex Fr.) Krummer] may attack the root systems of weakened trees more readily.

Changes in the Stand Environment. The gradual loss of ponderosa pine from the conifer mixture has resulted in an accumulation of standing snags which eventually blow down. This accumulation of fuel can be expected to sustain a hotter temperature during wildfires which would contribute to the loss of green trees by heat injury to the cambium. As the stand becomes more open, wind velocity within it may increase. The result of this change could range from increased windthrow to increased rate of fire spread (32).

One of the more subtle effects of the removal of the larger ponderosa pines is the elimination of moisture interception by fog drip (33). Fog drip on the windward side of ridges becomes increasingly important at the crests. For example, at Mt. Wilson in the San Gabriel mountains, the fog drip under the leeward side of a ponderosa pine was 60.27 inches compared with 27.23 inches in the open—more than 100% increase (33). Fogs occur frequently from late winter through June in the study area. The real significance of this increase of moisture to companion vegetation or the watershed is not well defined.

Preliminary Conclusions. The successional trends in ponderosa pine-sugar pine-fir forest cover type under chronic exposure to oxidant air pollution will vary greatly with the site. As ponderosa pine continues to decline in numbers—especially on the more exposed ridge crests—the conditions there will probably favor natural regeneration of shrub species more than the other conifers diminishing the recreational opportunities here. The resulting appearance may be similar to other nearby areas converted to brush by logging and fire. White fir may have a competitive edge over the remaining conifers on the more favorable sites on north-facing slopes. However, the present abundance of incense cedar in the understory suggests that stand management procedures try to enhance it in the immediate future, especially because it is more oxidant tolerant than white fir and may satisfy recreational needs.

The former typical appearance of the "mixed conifer forest" dominated by ponderosa pine will change in ways that may not enhance the recreational uses, wildlife habitat, and watershed values of the area. Repeated sanitation salvage treatment of damaged stands will eliminate the larger pines which might produce seed for natural regeneration and rapidly diminish the opportunity for any significant timber harvest in the future. Only a massive replanting program utilizing the more oxidant-tolerant species or selections, improved planting techniques, fuel management, and/or fire protection can ensure the maintenance of a forest cover in the future. This limited study of the conifer species composition and the oxidant damage to ponderosa pine suggests that more intensive research is needed in deciding how to properly manage the "mixed conifer forest" subjected to chronic photochemical oxidant air pollution.

Literature Cited

1. Miller, P. R., Parmeter, J. R., Taylor, O. C., Cardiff, E. A., *Phytopathology* (1963) **53,** 1072–1076.
2. Parmeter, J. R., Jr., Bega, R. V., Neff, T., *Plant Dis. Rep.* (1962) **46,** 269–273.

3. Society of American Foresters, "Forest Cover Types of North America (Exclusive of Mexico)," Washington, D. C., 1954.
4. Wert, S. L., *Proc. Intern. Symp. Remote Sensing Environ.*, 6th, 1969, pp. 1169–1178.
5. Miller, P. R., Millecan, A. A., *Plant Dis. Rep.* (1971) **55**, 555–559.
6. Horton, J. S., *U. S. Forest Serv., Tech. Paper* **44**, (1960).
7. Miller, P. R., McCutchan, M. H., Ryan, B. C., *Proc. Intern. Conf. Forest Experts Fume Damage, 1970.*
8. Miller, W. J., *Geol. Soc. Amer. Bull.* (1946) **57**, 457–542.
9. Parish, S. B., *Zoe* (1894) **4**, 322–352.
10. Stark, R. W., Miller, P. R., Cobb, F. W., Jr., Wood, D. L., Parmeter, J. R., Jr., *Hilgardia* (1968) **39**, 121–126.
11. Cobb, F. W., Jr., Stark, R. W., *J. Forest.* (1970) **68**, 147–149.
12. Miller, P. R., unpublished data.
13. Sischo, P. C., Calif. Div. Forestry (1958).
14. Fowells, H. A., *U. S. Dept. Agr., Handbook No.* **271**, (1965b).
15. Dunning, Duncan, *U. S. Dept. Agr., Bull.* **1176**, (1923).
16. Fowells, H. A., Schubert, G. H., *U. S. Forest Serv., Res. Note* **PSW-78**, (1951).
17. Schubert, G. H., *U. S. Forest Serv., Res. Note* **PSW-117**, (1956).
18. Fowells, H. A., Stark, N. B., *U. S. Forest Serv., Res. Paper* **PSW-24**, (1965).
19. Schubert, Gilbert H., *J. Forest.* (1955) **53**, 732.
20. Fowells, H. A., Schubert, G. H., *J. Forest.* (1951) **49**, 192–196.
21. Fowells, H. A., *U. S. Forest Serv., Res. Note* **PSW-41**, (1944).
22. Mitchell, A. J., *U. S. Dept. Agr., Bull.* **604** (1918).
23. Eaton, Charles B., *J. Forest.* (1941) **39**, 710–713.
24. Harward, M. R., Treshow, M., *Air Pollut. Contr. Ass., Preprint, 1971.*
25. Gordon, A. G., Gorham, E., *Can. J. Bot.* (1963) **41**, 1063–1078.
26. Miller, P. R., Parmeter, J. R., Flick, Brigitta H., Martinez, C. W., *J. Air Pollut. Contr. Ass.* (1969) **19**, 435–438.
27. Fowells, H. A., Schubert, G. H., *U. S. Dept. Agr., Tech. Bull.* **1150**, (1956).
28. Feder, W. A., *Science* (1968) **160**, 1122.
29. Adams, Lowell, *J. Forest.* (1955) **53**, 35.
30. Engle, R. L., Gabelman, W. H., *Proc. Amer. Hort. Sci.* (1966) **89**, 423–430.
31. Leonard, O. A., Hull, R. J., *Hilgardia* (1965) **37**, 115–153.
32. Countryman, C. M., *Proc. Soc. Amer. Forest. Ann. Mtg., 1955.*
33. Kittredge, J., "Forest Influences," McGraw-Hill, New York, 1948.

RECEIVED September 23, 1971.

10

Air Pollution and the Future of Agricultural Production

WALTER W. HECK

Southern Region, Agricultural Research Service, U. S. Department of
Agriculture, North Carolina State University, Raleigh, N. C. 27607

*Ozone and sulfur dioxide are presently the most pervasive
air pollutants affecting agricultural production. They have
a major impact on the growth and productivity of certain
sensitive cultivated and native species of plants. These
pollutants are a national problem around urban centers but
are important in rural areas, particularly throughout the
eastern United States. The present information base is too
diffuse to permit an accurate prediction as to the eventual
impact on agricultural production. Management practices
would permit us to live with present pollution levels, but a
decrease in these levels would be beneficial to agricultural
production. Doubling of present levels in the eastern part
of the country could result in major yield reductions of important agronomic crops. Long term chronic studies of field
problems are essential before an accurate assessment of the
impact of air pollutants on agricultural production can be
developed.*

Air pollution as presently defined involves many chemicals that are
released into the atmosphere through various human activities. The
most widespread and pervasive pollutants affecting agricultural production include ozone, sulfur dioxide, other oxidants, fluoride, and ethylene.
These gaseous pollutants have been relatively well studied and are known
to have a major impact on agriculture. Today many other materials are
also considered to be air pollutants that were not considered such a few
years ago. These include various trace elements released from manufacturing processes and present in exhaust gases, pesticides which are carried long distances as gases or as fine aerosols, and various gaseous
materials, such as ammonia and chlorine, released in accidental spills and

in manufacturing processes. In most cases we know little about these "new" air pollutants with respect to their impact on agricultural production. Thus, this paper is directed toward the pervasive gaseous air pollutants that are known to affect agricultural production. The general context of this paper also relates to those other "new" air pollutants if they are shown to be airborne over long distances and time and if they are detrimental to agricultural production. The paper does not discuss the effects of air pollutants on animals, animal communities, or wildlife, but it does include a broader coverage of effects on vegetation than is normally associated with agricultural interests.

A serious national air pollution problem exists today, particularly near large urban centers. Many believe this is a localized urban problem, and, in some parts of the country this may be true. There is evidence, however, that a severe regional problem exists throughout the eastern half of the United States, especially along the coast from North Carolina to Maine. Californians are well aware of the problems in their state and realize that air pollution is rapidly becoming a statewide problem, no longer isolated in the major metropolitan areas.

Researchers have mixed responses on the current extent of the air pollution problem in relation to its impact on vegetation. We know that injury occurs in many sensitive native and domestic plant species throughout the country. We do not know how severe the long term pollution effects will be on domestic species, on the frequency or distribution of native species, or on the complex interactions between native species and the effects of these interactions on plant communities. Much research is needed in this area before we can adequately speculate on the future of agricultural production.

This volume has been structured to develop a total concept of the known effects of air pollutants on plants. Thus, the other chapters discuss the basic regulatory mechanisms for plant growth and function; the known effects of air pollutants on plant chemistry; visible effects of pollutants, including both chronic and acute; the effects on growth and productivity; the effects on genetic patterns and the potential breeding programs to develop resistant varieties; and finally, plant communities and the influence of air pollutants on ecosystems. This chapter uses information from these other papers to show the interrelations of studies that are being conducted. These interrelations must be understood and evaluated in terms of present knowledge before the direction of future research can be determined. Such evaluations are also prerequisite to an understanding of air pollution and the future of agricultural production.

At the biochemical level of plant organization, *in vitro* studies have focused on the effect of air pollutants on isolated enzyme systems to determine the effects of such pollutants on specific enzymes and enzyme groupings; then enzyme systems from plant parts or whole plants have been studied after exposure of the plants to specific pollutants. Research has also focused on the next higher level of organization with both *in vitro* and *in vivo* studies on cell organelles and cell walls. Pollutants affect specific enzymes and enzyme systems that cause changes in bio-chemical reactions affecting metabolic pathways within the whole organism. Changes in metabolic pathways may directly or indirectly affect membrane integrity, resulting in the disruption of cellular organelles. Other direct or indirect changes may interfere with the metabolic function of certain organelles. Such effects could eventually cause reduced growth and/or cell death. At certain concentrations the cytoplasmic membranes are affected, resulting in an outward diffusion of water and solutes. When pollutant concentrations are high enough to produce acute injury, the effects on all membranes within plant cells, if not reversed or repaired, will produce cell death. Long term chronic pollutant effects are the result of the slow breakdown of various cellular components or the retardation of various synthetic reactions which lead to the loss of chlorophyll. These changes produce chlorosis, necrosis, and senescence of leaves and other plant parts. Changes also take place that do not produce externally visible symptoms but nevertheless affect growth, yield, and/or quality of the plant. If the outward symptoms are severe enough, death can result. If these effects to individual sensitive plants within a population are multiplied through the more resistant plants of a given cultivar or species, we may find cultivar or species death in cultivated agricultural crops or selections and eventual species death in complex natural ecosystems. With a reduction in vigor or demise of species and a continuing impact of air pollution, we start to see effects on plant communities and ecosystems. In the cultivated agricultural community, such as soybean or tobacco, these pollutant-induced effects could result in the loss of productivity, and eventually the crop would no longer be profitable to grow. In complex natural communities continued air pollution could have a marked effect on species frequency and could, with time, completely change community composition. Thus, research leads from effects on the fundamental systems within a single plant to effects on the most complex interrelationships of many plants within natural plant communities. Figure 1 is a flow diagram of the foregoing concepts.

Economics

The consequences of environmental pollution have not been intensively assessed. Some economists place an economic value on any aspect of an effect that may be important to man. If this comprehensive concept of economics is used, our ability to assess the true economic effects of pollutants on vegetation is just beginning.

The first survey to estimate the effects of photochemical air pollution on vegetation was developed in the mid-1950's (*1*) for some areas of California. This survey used estimates derived from visible injury and included several major crop types and a single category of weeds, as they responded to certain pollutants. Although the pollutant list was not inclusive, this survey was fairly comprehensive for the crops studied and the California counties included. This survey did not estimate a monetary loss for the area of California covered. However, economic loss predictions have since been based on this early survey following superficial visual estimates of injury in several agricultural areas. These superficial predictions fixed an annual loss of approximately 8 million dollars on the West Coast and 18 million dollars on the East Coast by the early 1960's for all types of pollutants (*2*). These estimates were then made countrywide, and yearly losses of between 200 and 500 million dollars have been suggested (*3*).

In 1969 (*4*) the state of Pennsylvania initiated a short training course for their county agricultural agents prior to a general survey of the state for damages to vegetation from air pollution. A year-long survey based on visual effects brought an estimated 11.5 million dollar loss for the state (*5*). This survey technique has since been adopted by California, New Jersey, the New England states, and the Extension Service of the Department of Agriculture.

A different type of economic study, initiated in 1969, used an empirical formulation to develop economic estimates of vegetation damage (*6*). On the thesis that hydrocarbon emissions are related to oxidant production, hydrocarbon emission data were collected from over 100 metropolitan areas in the United States. Reductions in crop yields were empirically related to these emissions, and the monetary values were calculated. The reliability of this technique was based on known effects of oxidants on crop species and on the known relationship between hydrocarbons and oxidants. There are disadvantages to the method used, and the results suffer from lack of field verification. However, the technique has obvious advantages such as ease of use and uniformity of results. It might be a prototype from which more accurate estimates can be developed. Results from two years of development are found in annual reports (*6, 7*) and show between 100–125 million dollars lost annually in the United States.

No method is available for predicting the economic loss to vegetation in the United States from air pollutants. Surveys to date have not found a way to incorporate the impact of pollutants on the growth and yield of crops where visible injury is not found or, if present, is not recognized. If these factors were included with the additional pollutant impact on ornamentals and on natural ecosystems, it would be reasonable to expect

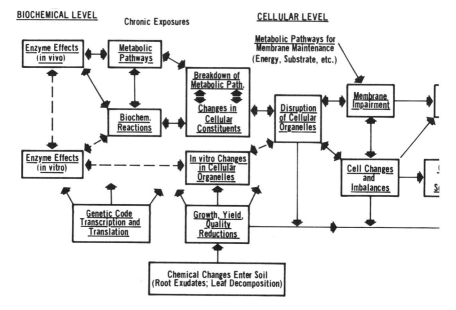

Figure 1.   Effects of air pollutants on plant

annual losses amounting to billions of dollars for vegetation alone. Parenthetically, these values, if used, would tacitly imply a major impact on presently unmeasured biological systems, as well.

What should be our point of departure for future research on the effects of air pollutants on vegetation? Is one level of the life system of vegetation more important to study than another? If air pollutants, over time, have no identifiable impact on an individual member of a species, the transitory changes which might be measurable at the biochemical level could be of no biological importance. If the pollutant has an effect on members of a species but this effect is random in nature and has no long term impact or no obvious impact on the plant community, it is probably not of major importance. However, if no observable impact can be found on plant communities at a certain level of pollutant occurrence within the atmosphere, then the pollutant is almost certainly of little importance.

Therefore, if no impact can be found in a plant community in terms of species composition, frequency, presence, total biomass, or quality of product after long term exposures to specific pollutants or pollutant complexes, the pollutant or pollutant complex is of no importance to the plant community at the ambient concentrations measured. Thus our final concern over air pollutants and their impact on vegetation should involve their effects on plant communities, whether simple or complex, domestic or natural.

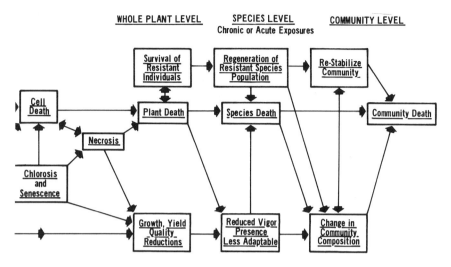

WHOLE PLANT LEVEL SPECIES LEVEL COMMUNITY LEVEL
Chronic or Acute Exposures

communities (chronic or acute exposures)

Plant Communities

If the plant community is the area of ultimate concern, then air pollution problems related to vegetation should be discussed in regard to plant communities. Three general types of plant communities are visualized: the single-crop agricultural community, the managed range and forest ecosystem, and the complex natural ecosystem. The single-crop agricultural community is discussed here from an historical perspective, and a general approach to a study of this type is outlined. The managed range and forest ecosystem and the complex natural ecosystem are discussed in relation to past approaches and general methods for future studies.

Tobacco is an example of a single-crop agricultural community on which the effects of ozone have long been recognized. The effects were referred to early as weather fleck on tobacco, but it was not until 1959 (8) that the causal agent was identified as ozone. In the late 1950's and early 1960's varieties of wrapper tobacco in the Connecticut valley and of flue-cured tobacco in Ontario, Canada, were severely injured by ozone, and continued production was threatened. Visible injury to the tobacco decreased both the quality and quantity of product.

It is difficult to assess accurately the effects of pollutants on yield and productivity when visible symptoms are present. It is presently impossible to determine effects on yield when injury is not recognizable because of the ubiquitous nature of air pollutants. Determination of the effects of ozone, with or without visible injury, has been attempted at the cellular level, on a whole-plant basis, and in some instances from a field or community approach. Most reports consider only the acute effects of ozone, as one part of the pollutant complex, on individual plants. A few studies have examined the long term, low level impact of specific pollutants or pollutant mixtures on the growth and yield of tobacco. These effects are difficult to prove under field conditions, but they have been shown by using special exposure-chamber designs for exposing the tobacco under greenhouse conditions. Research in the field suffers from the lack of unpolluted control sites that make it impossible to find comparable growing situations for both polluted and clean areas. At the present time field chamber research that does not permit easy comparison with field grown plants is the only feasible way to study the long term impact of air pollutants on field crops. It is possible that well described genetic material with known tolerance and susceptibility to specific pollutants or pollutant complexes could be compared in areas of high pollution or that protective sprays could be used for control plants. However, these are speculative and involve other problems.

One approach to community problems would involve several steps. A problem that affects one or more crop species is first identified in the field. Once a problem is recognized, the area is surveyed to identify injured species and obtain a list of possible pollutants. Selected species are screened by exposing them first to the individual pollutants and then to pollutant combinations to identify injury symptoms seen under field conditions. When the pollutant(s) are identified, the sensitive species are exposed to the pollutants at measured ambient concentrations on a long term basis under greenhouse conditions to determine effects on growth, yield, and/or quality. If significant effects are shown, the plants are tested under field conditions at a centralized location where pollutant concentrations can be controlled by exposure over varied times to determine whether similar effects also occur in the field. These field studies should be followed by studies at the sites where the problems are most prevalent. Special open-top field chambers (9) should be taken onto the sites to remove specific pollutants so that plants can grow normally in the field. Parts of all the above steps have been carried out in research locations around the world. The field-type studies are expensive, and the weaknesses and strengths have not been adequately explored; such studies of aspects of ecosystems involving crop production, however, are possible, have been done, and are profitable in terms of defining the ultimate effect of air pollution on agricultural production.

The effects of pollutants on managed range or forest ecosystems and the more complex natural ecosystems have not been studied as extensively as the simpler crop systems. Thus it is not known whether studies similar to those conducted with crops will yield information on the potential or actual impact of air pollutants on major ecosystems. This does not mean that the more complex systems have not been studied. Early studies concerned the single source sulfur dioxide emissions from smelters and the effects on surrounding vegetation. Perhaps the most extensive studies have been performed in relation to the smelters at Trail, British Columbia, Canada (*10, 11*), and in Sudbury, Ontario, Canada (*12, 13*). Most air pollution researchers in the United States are familiar with the little desert of Ducktown, Tenn., caused by sulfur dioxide emissions from a smelter (*14*). These and similar studies in Europe, North America, and Japan have focused attention on specific problem areas where the sources originated with no pollution-control devices. These local source problems are of less importance now because most sources have some form of control. Our present concern is more for the prevasive problems of the photochemical oxidants and sulfur dioxide from many sources or from high stacks with subsequent lower concentrations spread over wider areas. One such case is in the mountain recreational areas surrounding the Los Angeles basin where the oxidants are causing a serious problem to ponderosa and some of the other pines. The complexity of this problem is magnified because of the invasion of the ponderosa pines by bark beetles after the trees are weakened by air pollution. We still are not able to determine the total impact of the oxidant air pollutants on this ecosystem.

The most difficult studies involve ecosystems in areas of the country where the impact of pollution is more insidious and harder to recognize. Meaningful studies on the eventual impact of present levels of air pollution on selected native ecosystems will take at least 10 to 20 years. The studies are made more difficult because the pervasiveness of the pollution complex hinders the development of control areas where pollution is low or absent within a potential study area. A natural ecosystem study should encompass all aspects listed for a study of a single-crop community plus a major on-site field effort. Such a study was envisaged in west-central Pennsylvania where eight major study sites were selected within a 25 × 45 mile rectangle near three major power plants (*15*). Monitoring in the area showed oxidant concentrations, at some of the sites that were close to those of major eastern cities. The presence of sulfur oxides and nitrogen oxides is known, and low fluoride concentrations are suspect. These eight study sites were chosen for similarities in edaphic features, slope, availability of water, and ease of access. Plans called for extensive pollutant and meteorological monitoring at these sites. The growth of crop and forest species were to be measured over an 8–10 year period and correlated with measured environmental parameters. These studies were to be done in conjunction with greenhouse experiments, controlled field exposures of selected native vegetation, and a continuing survey of native vegetation in the experimental area. The inclusion of special field chambers for pollutant removal and large pot studies to reduce the edaphic variables was also planned. Although this project was terminated, such studies are necessary if we are to understand the insidious effects of air pollutants at concentrations where presently recognizable effects cannot be determined. Results of such studies are required before we can accurately predict the effects of air pollution on agricultural production.

Surveys of urban areas or areas around single pollutant sources have long been an accepted method of studying the impact of air pollutants on plant species and on ecosystems. These studies are no longer sufficient. This is not to say that useful information cannot be obtained from surveys of urban areas; the severity of observable problems in urban communities can be identified and mapped. If these observable effects could then be correlated with long term effects where symptoms are not identifiable, the total extent of the pollution problem within an urban situation could be derived from the surveys. However, the surveys alone will only identify the obvious and will prove inadequate to an understanding of the total impact.

Facts concerning pollutant impacts on ecosystems may be extrapolated from some laboratory and field investigations using native or cultivated plant species and combinations of species. It is possible, for instance, to determine whether air pollution affects the ability of native species to survive and compete. In a common forage pasture situation, such as ladino clover and fescue, air pollution may limit the growth of one crop, say clover, both from the direct effect on clover and through effects on fescue that in turn affect the growth of clover. Studies on such variables in specific phases and cohesive parts of ecosystems might yield information from which to extrapolate potential long term effects of pollutants on major ecosystems.

Certain adverse environmental conditions reduce the injurious effects of air pollutants on plants. This knowledge permits us to understand why plants in some parts of the country are more seriously affected by a given pollution level than others. This fact becomes more obvious when one notes the destructive impact of sulfur dioxide from smelters in Ducktown, Tenn., and the slight effect of smelters with similar emissions in the Southwest. Two factors interplay here—the type of vegetation and the arid environmental conditions. The Southwest has native plants which have adapted to arid conditions. These adaptive features apparently make many of these plants more tolerant to air pollutants. The arid conditions also induce tolerance even in sensitive plants. Thus visible injury around the southwestern smelters is associated primarily with irrigation practices and vegetation in and around stream beds. If these smelters were transported to the forest ecosystems of the East there would be many "Ducktowns." Although the humid East is under a photochemical "pall," a similar situation could arise if the concentrations of photochemical oxidants occurring in Los Angeles were to occur in the East. In this case, we would forecast major losses to both crop and native species.

Major studies of the effects of air pollutants on ecosystems are necessary, but ecologists have difficulty in relating changes in ecosystems to normal variations in meteorological and soil conditions. A procedure for such a major study has been developed by scientists in California through a contract with the Environmental Protection Agency. The beginning of an understanding of present levels of air pollution on complex ecosystems should come from this study.

Community studies must be approached from an effects modeling standpoint if any long term understanding of air pollution effects on ecosystems is to be attained. Although the concept of modeling is not new, it has not been used extensively to study air pollution effects on vegetation. O'Gara (*16*) developed a model to predict acute injury to plants from sulfur dioxide over short times. German workers (*17*) extended this with a model for both acute and long term fumigation studies for sulfur dioxide. We have published an equation (*18*) which predicts acute effects of pollutants on plant species where both time and concentration are independent variables. We are attempting to develop models that incorporate several pollutants and/or pollutant combinations as well as several important environmental parameters. It should be possible to develop an experimental model for an ecosystem based on simple modeling concepts from laboratory and field experimental work.

Future of Agricultural Production

The future of agricultural production is discussed with relatively little data base to work from and in the light of possible future levels of air pollution. We can visualize the situation in the eastern seaboard states for the photochemical oxidants and sulfur oxides. The following discussion assumes no major impact of other pollutants. However, they could be important.

Agronomic and other cultivated species would not be acutely impaired if future oxidant and sulfur dioxide levels remain as they are today. There appears to be sufficient genetic resistance to foliar injury within cultivated species that cultivars which are resistant to existing pollution levels can be developed. This does not mean that chronic symptoms would not develop under given conditions, nor that growth and yield reductions would not occur. Our understanding of these long term chronic effects is not sufficiently advanced for sound extrapolation, but it is probable that growth and yield reductions would occur. Many existing cultivars would have to be replaced, which would reduce the number of cultivars available for use. Effects on native vegetation are not sufficiently well documented for strong conjecture. It is possible that certain sensitive species that do not contain sufficient genetic plasticity might become extinct in this area. In general, the more sensitive variants in native species would not survive, but the more resistant variants would probably adapt and compete favorably in the native ecosystem.

If oxidant and sulfur dioxide levels decrease, agronomic and other cultivated species would show progressively less chronic injury and less reduction in both growth and productivity. In most, if not all, species an effects threshold probably exists below which the plant can detoxify the potentially harmful effects of an air pollutant with no detrimental effect to the plant. The same is true for native vegetation. The threshold for the most sensitive native variant of a species would be much lower than for cultivated plants which passed through a breeding program designed to increase tolerance to air pollutants. However, the genetic resistance qualities within the native plants should be as protective as those in cultivated species. The concentration which could be considered the threshold value for sensitive native plants is unknown, but it is probably somewhat under half of the present pollution level on the East Coast. Thus if present control plans cause a reduction in present oxidant and sulfur dioxide levels, agricultural programs should develop in a productive fashion.

The potential effect of an increase in oxidant and/or sulfur dioxide concentration is difficult to forecast. At some level the genetic resistance within a species is not sufficient to cope with a pollution insult. This level varies for both native and cultivated species. Once a given pollution level is reached, the effect may increase rapidly with only slight increases in pollution. An educated guess suggests that a doubling of present pollution concentrations on the East Coast could, under otherwise favorable environmental conditions, produce from 25 to 100% loss of many agronomic and horticultural crops and severe injury to many native species. Several growing seasons at these higher pollution levels could result in the temporary or permanent loss of native species and major changes in many ecosystems. We are not far from pollution levels which could cause precipitous effects on agricultural production in the more humid areas of the United States. However, an important variable must be considered in making any predictions based on increased pollution levels. This is that the capability of the living organism to respond and adapt to changes in its environment, within specific ranges of an adverse insult, has not been adequately determined.

Literature Cited

1. Middleton, J. T., Paulus, A. O., "The Identification and Distribution of Air Pollutants through Plant Response," *Arch. Ind. Health* (1956) **14**, 526–532.
2. Middleton, J. T., "Photochemical Air Pollution Damage to Plants," *Ann. Rev. Plant Physiol.* (1961) **12**, 431–448.
3. USDA, Agricultural Handbook, No. 291 (August 1965).
4. Lacasse, N. L., Moroz, W. J., Eds., "Vegetation Damage: Handbook of Effects Assessment," Center for Air Environment Studies, Pennsylvania State University, 183 pp., 1969.
5. Lacasse, N. L., Weidensaul, T. C., Carroll, J. W., "Statewide Survey of Air Pollution Damage to Vegetation—1969," Center for Air Environment Studies, Pennsylvania State University, *CAES Publ.* **148-70**, 52 pp., 1970.
6. Benedict, H. M., Olson, R. E., "Economic Impact of Air Pollutants on Plants," *Ann. Rept. SRI Project* **PHS-8115** (1970).
7. Benedict, H. M., Miller, C. J., Olson, R. E., "Economic Impact of Air Pollutants on Plants in the United States," *Ann. Rept. SRI Project* **LSD-1056** (1971).
8. Heggestad, H. E., Middleton, J. T., "Ozone in High Concentrations as Cause of Tobacco Leaf Injury," *Science* (1959) **129**, 208–210.
9. Heagle, A. S., Body, D. E., Heck, W. W., "An Open-Top Field Chamber to Assess the Impact of Air Pollution on Plants," *Jour. Environ. Quality*, in press.
10. "Effects of Sulfur Dioxide on Vegetation," National Research Council of Canada, Publ. **815** (1939).
11. Scheffer, T. C., Hedgcock, G. G., "Injury to Northwestern Forest Trees by Sulfur Dioxide from Smelters," *USDA Tech. Bull.* **1117** (1955).
12. Dreisinger, B. R., "Sulfur Dioxide Levels and the Effects of the Gas on Vegetation near Sudberry, Ontario," *Ann. Meet. Air Poll. Contr. Assoc., 58th, Toronto, Canada, June 21–24, 1965*, Paper 65-121.
13. Linzon, S. N., "Economic Effects of Sulfur Dioxide on Forest Growth," *J. Air Poll. Contr. Assoc.* (1971) **21**, 81–86.
14. Seigworth, K. J., "Ducktown—A Postwar Challenge. Can Man Correct a Century of Land Abuse in Tennessee's Copper Basin? A Start has been Made," *Am. Forests* (1953) **49**, 521–523; 553.
15. Heck, W. W., Weber, D. E., "Experimental Design of a Field Program to Determine the Effects of Large Coal Burning Power Plants on Vegetation," Forestry Commission (London), Research and Development Paper No. **82**, 16 (1971).
16. O'Gara, P. J., "Sulfur Dioxide and Fume Problems and Their Solutions," *Ind. Eng. Chem.* (1921) **14**, 744.
17. Guderian, R., van Haut, H., Stratmann, H., "Probleme der Erfassung und Beurteilung von Wirkungen Gasformiger Luftverunreinigungen auf die Vegetation," *Z. Pflanzenk. Pflanzenschutz.* (1960) **67**, 257–264.
18. Heck, W. W., Tingey, D. T., "Ozone. Time-concentration Model to Predict Acute Foliar Injury," *Proc. Intern. Clean Air Congr., 2nd, 1970*, Academic, New York and London, pp. 249–255, 1971.

RECEIVED September 23, 1971. This article is the result of cooperative investigations of the U. S. Department of Agriculture, the North Carolina State University, and the Environmental Protection Agency, Raleigh, N. C. 27607.

INDEX

INDEX